Compost This Book!

THE ART OF COMPOSTING FOR YOUR YARD, YOUR COMMUNITY, AND THE PLANET

BY TOM CHRISTOPHER
AND MARTY ASHER

SIERRA CLUB BOOKS • SAN FRANCISCO

The Sierra Club, founded in 1892 by John Muir, has devoted itself to the study and protection of the earth's scenic and ecological resources — mountains, wetlands, woodlands, wild shores and rivers, deserts and plains. The publishing program of the Sierra Club offers books to the public as a nonprofit educational service in the hope that they may enlarge the public's understanding of the Club's basic concerns. The point of view expressed in each book, however, does not necessarily represent that of the Club. The Sierra Club has some sixty chapters coast to coast, in Canada, Hawaii, and Alaska. For information about how you may participate in its programs to preserve wilderness and the quality of life, please address inquiries to Sierra Club, 730 Polk Street, San Francisco, CA 94109.

LIBRARY OF CONGRESS CATALOGING-IN-PUBLICATION DATA
Christopher, Thomas.
    Compost this book! / by Tom Christopher and Marty Asher.
      p. cm.
    Includes bibliographical references (p.   ) and index.
    ISBN 0-87156-596-X
    1. Compost. I. Asher, Marty. II. Title.
  S661.C45   1994
  631.8'75 — dc20   93–25659
                                                            CIP

Production by Janet Vail
Book and cover design by Paula Schlosser
Front cover illustration by Alexander Laurant
Inside illustrations by Karen Benson
Composition by Wilsted & Taylor

Printed in the United States of America

10   9   8   7   6   5   4   3   2   1

DEDICATION

To Matthew, Daniel, and Madeleine

We cleaned up after you — may this book help you clean up after us.

Contents

ACKNOWLEDGMENTS

Many individuals and organizations—too many, alas, to list individually—provided us with help and information in the course of this book's creation. We thank them all. In addition, we would like to extend special thanks to:

Suzanne—who never lost her sense of humor even when we threatened to feed her a compost-cooked meal

Joseph Spieler—agent, friend, and diplomat

The librarians of the New York Botanical Garden—is there any question they cannot answer?

THE MATERIALS IN THIS BOOK

Compost This Book! is printed with soy-based ink on recycled paper that contains 50% recovered waste by fiber content and 15% post-consumer waste by total weight. The paper is whitened without the use of dioxin-producing chlorine. The cover stock is recycled paper with 50% recovered waste by fiber content and 10% post-consumer waste by total weight. The book is compostable when properly prepared for the composting bin. Note that the cover and the binding go into the waste basket. See the Epilogue, page 226, for more information.

CHAPTER 1

From Lettuce to Lettuce

COMPOST. What does it want from me? Must I use the small part of my life that I *don't* spend working, worrying about how to dispose of the fruits of my labor? Compost. It's good for the roses, but it smells bad — or is that manure? And what's the difference anyway? You can compost in your backyard, but if the wind blows from the wrong direction your neighbors may kill you — or you may want to kill yourself first, right? Can't I choose to save the planet in one of the *other* fifty-six ways? Oh, yes, and what *is* compost?

Basically, compost is nothing less than the raw material for new life. Brown and crumbly — sometimes it's lumpy, more often it's fine and loose, sifting easily between your fingers — compost has the clean, fresh smell of the earth itself. Fueled by the sun's energy, plants transform minerals from the earth and gases from the air into living tissue, and once this dies and is broken down into its constituent parts, then it's compost—a priceless source of energy and building blocks for the next generation of plants.

As far as plant nutrients go, it's the main source, too. However, compost is not the ultimate fertilizer, no matter what the more zealous organic gardeners may claim. Compared to the chemicals you buy in a sack down at the garden center, compost provides only a very modest budget of nutrients. A typical bag of fertilizer, so-called 5–10–5, is fully 5 percent nitrogen, 10 percent phosphorus, and 5 percent potassium—and some synthetic fertilizers are even more concentrated, such as urea, which contains 42 percent soluble nitrogen, and calcium metaphosphate, which is 53 percent phosphoric acid (a phosphorus compound readily absorbed by plants). By comparison the best compost won't rate much more than 3.5–1–2, and a more typical yield for a homemade compost would be in the neighborhood of 1.5–0.5–0.5.[1]

Organic gardeners argue that there is qualitative difference between the nutrients supplied by compost and by synthetic fertilizers, and that plants actually get more benefit from feeding with compost. We'll look at those arguments in the next chapter. But it's worth noting that just by virtue of quantity alone, compost (both man-made and natural) is a far more important nutrient source than those chemicals we whip up with fossil fuels. One soil scientist has calculated that of the 350

---

[1]See Golueke, Clarence G., *Composting: A Study of the Process and Its Principles,* Emmaus, PA: Rodale Press, 1972, page 103. The nutrient levels in the finished compost depend principally on the richness of the materials added to the heap. As a result, the backyard bin, with its heady blend of food scraps and fresh, green wastes, generally turns out a better product than a municipal leaf or yard-waste pile.

million tons of nitrogen needed worldwide for crop and fodder production each year, 20 to 40 million tons are supplied by commercial fertilizers. An additional 10 tons are supplied by farmyard manures and green manures (crops grown solely for their fertilizer value and turned back into the soil). All the rest, as much as 300 million tons, comes from the decay of organic matter in the soil. Compost is what feeds us, too, whether we realize it or not.

But compost gives far more to the soil than nutrients. The humus it supplies improves the structure of the soil, making it lighter and yet more absorbent; humus also slows soil erosion; and it restores topsoil. Indeed, a single, generous dose of compost can add as much topsoil to your plot as nature would take a century to accumulate. That's why compost is the ideal medicine for any wornout or otherwise mistreated earth.

Compost is also remarkable for its cleansing power. Made from virtually anything that was once alive — weeds, manure, even old eggshells and tea bags — finished compost is so clean that when added to the soil, it protects plants — and your family, too — from all sorts of diseases, parasites, and toxins. That's why composting is an ideal way to reduce the flow of garbage that is threatening to bury us alive. Sanitation engineers say that more than 60 percent of our solid waste is compostable (see Chapter 3) — and once it is composted, everybody is going to want it in the backyard.

In short, the benefits you get from composting are simply the reward for working *with* nature rather than against it.

How does the process work? It's degrading, degradation in an accelerated form — at least that's what the scientists call composting. Actually, there's much about this process scientists don't understand. "Biodegradation" is a well-established field with congresses, textbooks, and all the usual scholarly apparatus. But what biodegradationists have traditionally studied has been *stopping* decay. They do this very effectively, and can offer sound advice on everything from keeping termites out of timber to keeping latex paint mildew free. But when it comes to *enhancing* rot, they are much less savvy.

That's unfortunate, since in the natural scheme of things decay is far more important than preservation. If it were not for decomposers—the insects and microorganisms that attack and digest organic matter—most of the soil- and air-borne nutrients that plants assemble into their tissues, and the energy they take from sunlight and store there, would be lost once the plants died. But because of decomposers, death is not a dead end, only a step toward more life.

This emerged clearly from a study of a New Hampshire forest: the ecologists found that roughly 75 percent of all the new organic matter—leaves, twigs, seeds, and roots—produced by the woodland plants died within the first year and fell to the ground. A small portion of this—a little more than 4 percent—stayed on the forest floor to build the reserve of organic debris. The rest was released back into the forest ecosystem through decomposition. The fuel for new growth produced in this fashion each year equaled almost three-quarters as much as all the sunlight plant leaves were able to trap during that period.

Think of it as inconspicuous consumption. Probably you don't live in a forest, but even so, biodegradation goes on all around you. You just don't notice it—except if, rooting around in the refrigerator, you come on a lettuce you stashed in the crisper three weeks ago. Then your only comment is probably a curse, followed by a dunk shot into the trash can. Who *wants* to know what's living in that slimy black mess!

If you swallowed your disgust, however, and looked really closely (you'd need a microscope for this) you'd find a veritable universe of curious creatures and plants there. If you left the lettuce outside for a week or two more, you'd find these scavengers joined by a host of larger decomposers, creatures just barely visible to the naked eye. There'd be a whole ecosystem in miniature lurking in that geriatric vegetable.

Ecologists call it a "food web," this jostling crowd of earthworms, millipedes, mites, beetles, springtails, sow bugs, and snails. It's not unusual to identify a thousand different species of soil animals in the organic litter of a square meter of forest floor, and nearly all of these would be just as happy in the leaves piled up under your rhododendrons, or in a heap of kitchen refuse. Don't worry about these creatures inviting themselves in, though. Away from the soil, the outdoor decomposers would die as fast as a fish out of water.

Even if the larger decomposers are more spectacular, it's the microorganisms that do the real work of degradation. These are not "germs"; they are simple bacteria, fungi, molds, tiny mongrels called *actinomycetes* that are half fungi and half bacteria, and specialized protozoa, all of which feed only on dead plant tissue. They are tiny and simple, but they have the ability to digest the complex organic molecules such as cellulose that are useless in their original form to other animals and plants.

Maybe at this point the idea of attracting this invisible army to your yard is beginning to worry you. But it's too late, because they are already there, ready and waiting to recycle your lettuce for you. These scavengers are found nearly everywhere, and in inconceivable numbers. The same woodland soil that hosts a thousand species of animals per square meter typically supports 10 to 100 *million* bacteria per cubic centimeter. Soils poor in organic materials—the type you find in a

FIGURE 1. Guess who's coming to dinner? Chances are you'll find all of these (and many more) feasting on the left-overs in your compost heap (clockwise from the extreme left):

Springtail—Catapults around heap with its spring-loaded tail; 3,500 species. May eat compostables, or may eat the fungi that eat the compostables. Either way, takes organics one step closer to stable humus.

Actinomycetes—Mold-like bacteria that quickly spread thread-like gray mycelia throughout the heap. Especially effective at attacking tough, raw plant tissues, softening them up for less enterprising relatives.

Millipede—Consumes and processes raw plant material, leaving droppings that in turn feed bacteria and fungi.

Protozoan—Eats the bacteria that eats the wastes, one of the last steps in the decomposition process.

Fungus—One of the hardest-working decomposers, fast-growing and able to digest decay-resistant cellulose. With 50,000 species to choose from, there's a fungus for any material, any heap.

Land snail—Not a major decomposer itself, this creature assists process by chewing up larger plant wastes, turning them into smaller particles more accessible to bacteria and fungi.

Sowbug—An eater of compostables, but even more important as a means of transportation: bacteria and fungi hitch rides around the heap on its back.

Earthworms—Help aerate heap with their tunnels, and mix its contents as they pull materials into the interior.

yard that has been put on the "chem-lawn" habit, for instance — support fewer decomposers. That's why the thatch of dead grass blades and roots there doesn't rot away, and why you have to pay the landscaper to rake it up and haul it away. But even chem-lawn isn't decomposer free.

Only extremely cold-climate regions like the arctic tundra are truly inhospitable to these microorganisms; they don't flourish at low temperatures. That's the principle behind your refrigerator, of course, that and the fact that you seal your food in air-tight containers before you set it down on the refrigerator shelf. Most decomposers are aerobic organisms — that is, they need oxygen to survive. There are anaerobic decomposers (decomposers that thrive without oxygen), but unfortunately they are the ones that make the lettuce stink. Their digestion is poor, inefficient and incomplete; they are as gassy as any other greedy eater, filling the air around themselves with clouds of ammonia and hydrogen sulfide (the gas that gives rotten eggs their characteristic odor). Luckily, that's a bad habit that isn't shared by the *aerobic* decomposers in a healthy compost heap; they leave only a sweet, clean odor.

There's one other place where decomposers don't flourish, and that, sadly, is the dump. To protect the surrounding groundwater and the noses of nearby residents, we line our landfills with clay and seal them with soil. There's even less oxygen here than in your refrigerator and very little moisture. Every living thing — even that aloe that has been gathering dust, forgotten, on the bathroom shelf for a couple of years — needs moisture, and decomposers won't find it in the heart of a dump. The result is that garbage entombed in a landfill stinks and lasts a long, long time.

In fact, according to archaeologists William Rathje and Wilson Hughes of the University of Arizona, even the most perishable products may survive many decades. These two scholars, who specialize in the study of modern garbage, have excavated landfills from Tempe to Staten Island, using the same meticulous techniques other archaeologists apply to ancient cities and cemeteries. Along with the statistics about different types of refuse they have gathered (Phoenix buries $6 million worth of recyclable aluminum every year; newspapers occupy 10.5 percent of the San Francisco landfill) has come the disturbing news that it doesn't much matter whether a plastic bag is biodegradable or not once we send it to the dump. The newspapers that the Garbage Project exhumed in San Francisco were, for the most part, perfectly legible after fifty years. Even food debris, they have found, degrades painfully slowly in a landfill, losing only 25 percent of its bulk over the first fifteen years, and with little or no change after that for the next four decades.

In your backyard, though, with only a small investment of time and work, you and your decomposers can reduce those same leftovers — lettuce and all, even newspapers — to valuable compost in as little as six weeks. If you aren't willing to make any special effort, that's OK; you can still have compost, and compost that's even better in some respects (see, in Chapter 6, the discussion of "slow" versus "fast" compost). You'll just have to wait longer, maybe six months, maybe even a year.

In either case, all it takes to make compost is an inconspicuous corner (because even if composting is a praiseworthy and profitable occupation, it isn't a visual treat) and some understanding about what decomposers want out of life (not much, actually).

They want organic materials on which to feed. More specifically, they need both carbon-rich compounds like cellulose as a source of energy, and nitrogen-rich stuff like manure, grass clippings, or ammonia as raw

material for the proteins they use to grow and reproduce. Give them these in roughly the right proportions
(it's easy—we'll tell you how to do that in Chapter 6)
plus the minerals and other "micronutrients" they
need in trace amounts (found in virtually any vegetative
waste), and they'll go to work.

They also need heat. The exact temperature they
prefer depends on the type of decomposer. There are
psychrophiles ("cold-loving") decomposers that prefer
temperatures of around 55°F; they will start their work
during the frosty months from late fall through early
spring. There are the mesophiles, "medium-tempera-
ture-loving" decomposers that flourish between 70°
and 90°F, and thermophilic ("heat-loving") ones that
bask in temperatures from 112° to 150°F. In any case,
you don't have to heat the compost; the microorganisms generate their own heat as they release the energy
locked up in your rotten lettuce or other organic debris.
All you have to do is to heap enough debris together so
that your pile is self-insulating. Then the psychrophiles
will go to work, producing the heat necessary to wake
the mesophiles (in the heat of summer, the heap will
skip this step). The mesophiles, in turn, will heat the
core of the heap until the thermophiles take over there;
the mesophiles and psychrophiles will continue to operate in the cooler, outer layer.

Keep a thermometer handy, and you will find that
the temperature of the compost heap provides a clue to
what is happening at the microscopic level. The heap
starts out at the same temperature as the surrounding
air, which is best for the psychrophiles and mesophiles,
but if you've managed an acceptable carbon–nitrogen
(fuel–nutrient) mix, the mercury begins to rise within
a few days until, within a week or ten days, the heap
crests at 150°F. You'll know that the thermophilic bacteria are busy then. They are the workhorses of biodeg-

radation; in contrast to the mesophiles, that number a few measly millions per pinch of compost, the thermophiles take reproduction seriously and soon make a population of 10 *billion* per gram of debris. Not only are they numerous, they are productive, and it's their presence that makes the difference between composting that is finished in six weeks and composting that takes a year or more. Indeed, they'll burn themselves out within three to five days unless you take steps (described in Chapter 6) to keep them going.

As the temperature within the heap drops, the mesophiles move back to the fore, and when it drops finally to ambient temperature, the composting process is complete. Incidentally, if you are the sort who hates technology, simply thrusting your hand into the center of the heap will tell you if the thermophilic decomposers are at work, though if they are really busy you may get scalded. Marty, who is both a technophobe and a coward, has another method. He relies on the neighbor's cat, at least during the cooler months. When Marty's heap is really cooking, the sybaritic creature is nearly always stretched out on top, luxuriating in the warmth. When she slips back to her house, it signals the composting is done.

Finally, as we've learned from the failure of our landfills, there are two more things that the desirable decomposers need—oxygen and water. They are easy enough to provide, and we'll tell you how in Chapter 6, where we describe in detail different ways to manage the heap. The organic materials you add to your heap, and the way you assemble them, will also affect the composting's progress. But keep in mind that composting is an extremely forgiving process, and anything smaller than a 2-ton tractor trailer will eventually break down into its component parts, given enough time (actually, given *unlimited* time, the semi will as well). This rule—perhaps the only hard and fast Law of Composting—is completely foolproof and immutable, except for one grapefruit that Marty's daughter threw into his compost pile on January 4, 1990, and which at the time of this writing is still perfectly identifiable with its "A&P Special 3 for 99 cents" sticker hideously intact. It is currently on submission to the *Guinness Book of Records*.

Man, of course, is never content to leave well enough alone, and while two centuries to break down a grapefruit may be fine for mother nature, you'll probably want to speed the process along. So later on we will look at the keys to more efficient composting: achieving a good blend of carbon and nitrogen, shredding, making sure there's enough air and water in the heap — and other tips for making composting as easy as, well, *not* composting.

What Is Humus, and What Is Organic Matter—and What's the Difference?

You will find these two terms all throughout this book, since you can't write about composting and avoid them. That's unfortunate, because using them lands us right in the middle of a nasty argument.

Gardeners tend to use these terms interchangeably, and many composters follow their lead. Scientists insist there is a difference, but can't agree on exactly what it is. To escape this swamp of confusion, we're going to stick our linguistic necks out, and establish our own definitions right now.

Organic matter includes anything in the soil that is living or has been living. Some authorities don't like to include in this category anything that's still crawling, but that's ridiculous. Maybe you don't want to include in your soil's organic content the chipmunk who has a hole under the woodpile. But if your soil is reasonably fertile, an acre of it will support 11,900 pounds of microorganisms—bacteria, fungi, and so forth. They are there to stay, too, and eventually will decompose themselves to add their bit to the general fertility. So include 'em, we say, along with all the plant roots, the fallen leaves and twigs, the dead and rotting plant and animal materials.

Humus is organic material, but it's organic material of a special kind. It's organic material in the last stage of decomposition, the stage right before the organic material breaks down into nonorganic chemical products such as carbonic acid, ammonia, and water. Humus ranges in color from brown to black—it's what gives fertile soils their dark color. It is amorphous, too; it's shapeless, and preserves none of the original structure of the leaves, twigs, or other materials.

Garden centers will sell you peat moss or animal manures as humus, which they are not—though they may become humus after they finish decomposing. But what about your compost—is it organic material or humus? It begins as organic material and, if you manage the heap properly, it should end up largely humus. When the heap cools and stops shrinking, when you can no longer recognize any of the debris you stuffed into it, then the heap has completed the transformation.

All humus is good for the soil, but scientists (in their hair-splitting way) like to distinguish different types of humus one from another. Actually, the motive for this isn't simply to bewilder the crowd. The exact formula of the humus—which seems to depend mostly on the type of decomposers that produce the material—drastically affects its stability in the soil. Some humuses you may add to your garden break down within weeks or months, but as one compost maven told Tom, other humuses may last thousands of years. Through the use of carbon$_{14}$ dating, he had determined that there are humuses that persist for thousands of years. There are humuses in our soil, he pointed out in a tone of awe, that were there when Christ walked the earth.

Aspergillus Fumigatus

It was Marty who mentioned nervously one day that he had learned there was a personal risk attached to composting. He'd been hearing rumors of some disease that struck down composters. Sure enough, a check of the literature revealed that composting vegetable waste *is* a haven for a parasitic mold known as *Aspergillus fumigatus*.

When Tom looked up the epidemiology of that pathogen, he was, initially, horrified. In language as chilling as it was clinical the textbooks warned that if this mold should invade your body, it may, God forbid, form hairy balls in your lungs. Severe cases, the books warned, may necessitate a lobectomy (and whatever that is, it doesn't sound good).

Then Tom read that while *Aspergillosis* can afflict humans, in practice it is a disease chiefly of penguins. Growing up in the antiseptic Antarctic, these birds cannot cope with the air they must breathe when moved to our zoos — and apparently *Aspergillus fumigatus* is everywhere in temperate climates. In a survey of American homes, one team of researchers found it in 85 percent of basements, 42 percent of bedrooms, and 56 percent of bathrooms. We figure that staying upstairs wouldn't be so bad, but that giving up the bedroom would be even worse than giving up the compost heap, and that avoiding the bathroom would create a health hazard worse than any fungus.

Anyway, a clinical study has also found that infection is no more common among compost plant workers than among the general population—that is, exceedingly rare. Unless you are a writer (they are all hypochondriacs), you can stop worrying.

Ten Intelligent Answers to Ten Stupid Questions You've Always Been Meaning to Ask About Compost

Q. What does it look like?

A. That depends to some degree on what you've chosen to compost. Autumn leaves, for example, will stay flaky even after they are ready to spread on the lawn or garden, while kitchen waste—coffee grounds, vegetable peelings, and so on—breaks down into coarse black granules. Eventually, composting will reduce anything to a pile of loose brown or black crumbs. If you want a sample, go to the woods and dig down through the mat of leaves that covers the ground until—right on top of the soil—you reach leafmold. That incredibly rich, moist, black stuff, like the crumbs of a German chocolate cake, is nature's compost.

Q. Does it smell?

A. Sure, everything smells. But compost doesn't smell like garbage, or manure, or even gooey, rotten lettuce. It smells like good, clean earth.

Q. Is compost the same as mulch?

A. No. A mulch is any material that gardeners spread in a blanket over the soil to keep it moist and weed free. Since compost will help the growth of virtually any plant, including weeds, it won't work for that purpose. Effective mulches include everything from sheets of plastic to peanut shells; the advantage of organic mulches such as peanut shells, shredded bark, or grass clippings is that eventually they compost themselves, rotting away to help enrich the soil. Plastic, of course, lies there forever, getting more tattered and ugly but never completely degrading.

Q. Does a compost heap attract animals?
A. Not if you use your head and add only plant debris to the heap. If you fill it full of meat scraps and bones, it certainly will attract the neighbor's mutt and maybe a family of raccoons, or even worse. But even then, once the composting process is complete, the finished product would be sterile and attractive only to plants.[2]

Q. Does it attract bugs?
A. Yes, but only good ones. When you shovel the finished compost into a wheelbarrow, you'll probably disturb a few sow bugs and millipedes, maybe a handful of earthworms. You may find a few fruit flies, too, hanging around the heap if you have added fruit or vegetable scraps recently and left them lying on top of the heap. But fruit flies aren't pests outdoors, where they can't get to your fruit bowl. What you won't find in a properly managed compost heap are roaches, mosquitoes, or termites — a hard-working heap is so full of decomposers that there isn't room there for the undesirables of the insect world.

Q. So how can I tell when the compost is finished and ready to use?

---

[2]A correspondent from central Maine has informed us that porcupines come to *his* heap to steal the vegetable parings. Should he stop composting vegetable scraps, too? Absolutely not! Our suggestion is that if your heap is infested with porcupines, continue to add vegetable scraps (so who wants a yard full of angry porcupines?) but in addition dump in the heap *lots* of meat scraps, too. That should attract all the neighbors' dogs and cats. Hopefully, the ensuing battle will (1) rid the neighborhood of stray pets, and (2) leave the porcupines stripped of quills so that you can safely put them in the trunk of your car and take them to a distant state park.

A. Volume provides one clue: by the time your heap of organic refuse has finished composting, it will have shrunk by about half. By that time, the temperature inside the heap will have dropped back to ambient and you won't be able to distinguish any of the original materials—if you can still recognize the rind of the cantaloupe you had for breakfast two months ago, or the maple leaves you raked up last fall, then the compost isn't ready yet.

In any case, don't try to hurry the process. Spreading the organic wastes over the garden before degradation is completed certainly won't harm you or the wildlife and it won't cause any lasting problems, but it may not be in the best interest of your plantings. Immature compost will temporarily absorb much of the soil's nutrients and although it will release these later as it finishes decomposition, that can leave plants hungry in the short term—unless you resort to store-bought fertilizers. Anyway, you probably won't like the way your garden looks when strewn with half-digested cantaloupes. But if you do make a mistake of this sort, take heart. The damage (if any) will be minor and time will provide the cure, as the organic materials continue to decompose on their own.

Q. Do you need a permit?
A. Only if you use your compost heap to cleanse your soil of toxic waste (as the Army is doing—see Chapter 5), or if you use composting to solve your community's solid waste disposal problems (see Chapter 9) so that you measure the finished compost in truckloads, not bushel baskets.

Q. Do I have to order one of those fancy (and expensive), rotating contraptions from Sweden?
A. The only thing you must have for making compost is garbage, although a pitchfork and a shovel are a help.

Many composters like a bin, because it hides the rotting compost from view and protects it from rain, which can drown the decomposers and slow the process, besides washing nutrients out of the finished product. But you can easily make your own bin from a roll of snow fencing, a length of chicken wire, or even a half dozen bales of hay (you'll find plans for these and several others in Chapter 7); you can also skip the bin and make your compost in a hole in the ground, or just a free-standing heap. For technology addicts who must have the right gadget for every task, Chapter 7 also offers a consumer's guide to composting accessories.

FIGURE 2. A technophobe's clue to compost maturity, Marty's thermophilic feline.

Q. Does it take a lot of time?

A. Yes, but not a lot of *your* time. Even if you hurry the decomposers, they still can't digest a heap of compostables in much less than six weeks. If you're a type A personality, like Tom, then you'll spend a lot of time going out to check on the heap, to read the thermometer and peer at the steam that rises from the heap when you jab at its top. If you're a type Z (for zzz's), like Marty, you'll wander back there every few weeks and poke it with a stick, or, better yet, have one of your ecologically eager children do it. But a cursory check once a week is more than enough.

Q. Does it take a lot of work?

A. Not if you are patient. If, like Marty, you are content to wait six months or a year while the decomposers do the work for you, you can stack the compostable materials in a heap and then forget about them until it's time to haul the finished compost away. If you are impatient, like Tom, and want to accelerate the decay, this will involve a modest investment of labor; that is, shredding the materials before you stack them and then stirring up the heap with a pitchfork once or twice. Even so, you'd probably have to work longer and harder to earn the money it would cost to haul the leaves and rubbish away, and to pay for the peat moss, fertilizer, and mulch you'd have to buy for your lawn and garden.

CHAPTER 2

A Brief History

COMPOST WAS INVENTED by a man named Obadiah R. Compost on Arbor Day in the year 1642, when he threw a squash out the window in a fit of pique and hit a raccoon. The following spring he noticed that neither the squash nor the raccoon was present but the roses he had planted in the spot grew to unprecedented height.

But seriously, folks. . . .

Compost has been around just about as long as life on earth. In fact, the process of composting provided the bacteria and fungi out of which life probably originated. The only reason compost seems a bit exotic to us now is because in the last few decades it has become the victim of our incessantly waste-producing society. Recently, because of increased ecological awareness and rising living costs, throwing things away unnecessarily has become unfashionable, expensive, often illegal, and generally uncool (just try and trash an egg carton

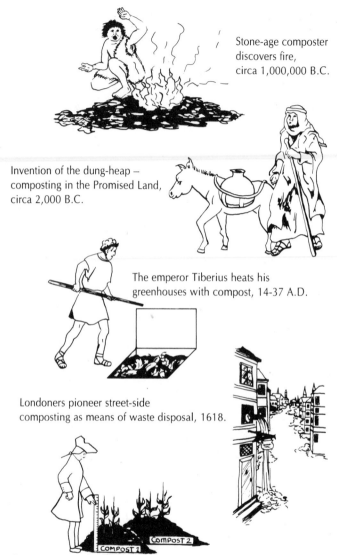

Stone-age composter
discovers fire,
circa 1,000,000 B.C.

Invention of the dung-heap —
composting in the Promised Land,
circa 2,000 B.C.

The emperor Tiberius heats his
greenhouses with compost, 14-37 A.D.

Londoners pioneer street-side
composting as means of waste disposal, 1618.

The Father of Our Compost Heap:
George Washington tests compost formulas and their effect on plants, 1760.

FIGURE 3. A composter's time-line: high points of the heap
from paleolithic to democratic.

in Marty's house). Recycling is a daily part of more and more households, and composting is simply do-it-yourself recycling. We've been looking for ways to live more lightly on the earth. So because it is so earth friendly and economically sensible, compost has now returned with a vengeance (not really a vengeance — compost is so friendly and benign, it has returned with a hug and a "Howdy, glad to see you again!").

The origins of compost lie far back in the lost, hidden recesses of prehistory. Some 350 million years ago, the continents and islands were covered with bare rock. As the first primitive plants moved in from the sea and tentatively established themselves on the shoreline, they drew their sustenance from mineral and rock particles. Their roots broke down some of the rock structure, and then they added their own skeletons to the mix. Year after year, century after century, eon after eon, the soil grew richer, allowing for the flourishing of a greater variety of plants.

Eventually, man came along. And, of course, he had to discover fire because without fire there would be no quiche or French fries, let alone civilization. The composting process, as we shall see, produces heat. And composting is inextricably linked with the development of fire. Although some anthropologists link man's use of fire to events such as lightning or volcanoes, others place it much closer to home. One theory has it that ancient tribes used to sleep in common beds that were heaps of leaves, grasses, and other organic stuff. These heaps were soft and since they furnished a perfect environment for bacteria, the prehistoric mattress generated lots of heat as it decayed. Periodically, the composting beds of our prehistoric ancestors may have spontaneously burst into flame (no doubt while two Neanderthals were making love).

One argument cited in favor of the "compost

school of fire discovery" is that it did not require a lot of intelligence to understand the usefulness of fire this way, since its warmth was already permeating the cave. And Neanderthal man was simply not very smart—his cranial capacity was closer to that of apes than to modern man (with the exception of Dan Quayle). The lightning or lava schools require somewhat more of a leap of imagination. Once the fire was already in the cave, it would be a simple step to invent such things as clay ovens. Besides, as late as this century some African tribes were seen to obtain fire from the rotting vegetables left by receding flood waters.

The first civilizations thrived in three regions: the Mesopotamian, Indus, and Nile valleys. Each of these locations possessed flat, fertile earth and an adequate, though not overly abundant, amount of rainfall. A surplus of tillable soil developed, which allowed farmers to farm the same plots for many generations — especially in an area like the Nile Valley, where yearly floods rejuvenated the land with nutrients. When the land finally did become depleted, as a result of overfarming, so did the civilization.

After a few million years of mindless meanderings, humanity got a brilliant idea—it may have been inspired by watching rivers dump new mud in fields. Rather than move every time the land wore out, perhaps there were ways the land could be enriched so that people could farm the same spot indefinitely.

Unfortunately, at least from an archeologist's point of view, some of these prehistoric farmers seem to have interpreted composting pretty broadly. Random scatterings of building rubble and other artifacts over surrounding fields suggest that early Mesopotamians regarded decayed houses and palaces as just another kind of compost. So as they fortified their crops, they consumed their own history.

One day, however, some prehistorical genius noted

that the grass grew greener not on the other side, as was commonly suspected, but where the cows did their business. Not only did manure prove superior to building rubble as a fertilizer, but it was easier to spread over the fields. So from then on, agriculture became manure obsessed.

Exactly when this first green revolution kicked off isn't clear, but a reference to the use of manure as fertilizer has been found in clay tablets of the Akkadian empire, a Mesopotamian kingdom that flourished (organically, of course) 2,300 years before the birth of Christ.

When fresh from the beast, manure isn't compost. But it contains all the necessary ingredients: lots of mashed and digested vegetable matter; an abundance of nitrogen and carbon and the bacteria necessary for decay. Now if farmers use manure in any quantity, they must first gather and stack it; if the manure is wet or as soon as it is moistened by some rain shower, it heats up and begins to decompose. At that point it ceases to be just . . . . waste . . . . and becomes compost. So really, the invention of the dung heap marked the invention of composting too.

Akkadians weren't the only Middle Easterners to note the value of dung ("protocomposting," we might call it, in the best academic tradition). The Talmud, the ancient Hebrew guide to everything from selling a goat to having sex, also speaks about this matter: "They lay dung to moisten and enrich the soil, dig about the roots of trees; pluck up the suckers; take off the leaves; sprinkle ashes and smoke under the trees to kill vermin."

The Greeks, who claimed to have invented everything worth having or doing, created a myth to explain how they had discovered composting. It centered around their strong, but not too bright hero Hercules. As penance for having murdered his own family, Hercules agreed to perform twelve tasks, or "labors." Number six was to clear away in one day all the dirt that had accumulated in the giant stables of Augeas, king of Elis. Hercules accomplished this by diverting a river and using its water to flush the building clean. Sadly, the Greeks didn't bother to record what effect this had on the crops in the flood plain.

But Homer, the Greeks' great epic poet, did refer in the *Odyssey* to "the mule and cow dung that had been saved in a heap for hauling to the field," and to the manuring of the vineyard that belonged to Odysseus' father. Some 500 years later, in the fourth century B.C., Theophrastus, "the father of botany" (Who was the mother? The Greeks never told you that) recommended not only the manuring of poor soils, but also the mixing in of animal bedding from the stable. That's a rough-and-ready sort of composting. And Theophrastus' fellow Athenians (a group notorious all over the Mediterranean for their sharp practice) operated the world's first commercial composting venture, selling the city's sewage to farmers for use as fertilizer.

The Romans had a number of important contributions to make to the new science besides being the first to compost Christians and an occasional slow lion. A man named Lucius Junius Moderatus Columella goes down in history as the person who raised composting to the level of science. In his twelve-volume guide to farming, *De Re Rustica,* he even gives a formula for a compost made without manure. If farmers had no obliging herd of animals, they could still make food for their crops (according to Columella) by mixing leaves of any sort of weeds, or even ferns and brambles, with straw, the sweepings of the barnyard, and ashes. This blend they should dump in a pit, moisten, and leave to decompose—and to keep serpents from hiding in this mess, the farmer should drive into its center a stake of oak wood.

Yet if he shared a vegetarian recipe with his readers,

this did not reflect any aversion to animal droppings. In fact, Columella was a self-confessed connoisseur of composted dung. In his book, he included a comparative rating of dove, goose, duck, and pigeon manures, as well as the usual cow, goat, and pig. Of the four-legged animals, Columella preferred the donkey as a source of dung, since he believed that stubborn beast chewed its food most thoroughly, thus giving the compost a head start. Columella also recognized the importance of composting all these materials thoroughly, so that any weed seeds should be killed. Finally, Columella was the first writer to come out of the closet (the water closet, that is) and hail the benefits human urine could provide to the compost heap. (Lucius, what are you doing out there in the garden?)

The emperor Tiberius decreed a new application of composting when his doctor prescribed a diet of cucumbers. To keep the vines in production right through the winter, the imperial gardeners planted them in pits covered with sheets of translucent talc and loaded with composting manure. The gardeners knew that as the manure decomposed it would generate heat as a by-product and they relied on this, together with the talc cover, to keep the frost away.

Composting, like most everything else, managed to survive the Dark Ages through the writings of learned Arabs. They recommended the superiority of human blood and crushed bones to be mixed with ash and lime for compost. We need not ask the details of how they obtained their supply.

Omar Khayyam, the Persian poet, wrote in the eleventh century,

> I sometimes think that never blows so red
> The rose as where some buried Caesar bled.

The Christian monasteries also share the credit for keeping composting alive throughout this dreary period. When not illuminating manuscripts or practicing Gregorian chant, the monks were liable to be out working in the fields, since most monasteries depended on attached estates for income as well as groceries. Maintaining the fertility of the soil was for the monks a part of being a good steward of God's gifts; it also meant more money in the coffers. So cleanliness might be next to godliness, but composting wasn't far behind— one old English abbey even installed conduits that drew the murky water from the fish pond to flush the monastic sanitation system and wash the whole organic-rich brew into the compost heap.

Not all uses of compost were approved, however, as Albertus Magnus (1193–1280) — bishop of Ratisbon and the medieval Church's greatest theologian, philosopher, and scientist— discovered to his sorrow. His success at reviving the Roman practice of using compost to force fruits and flowers out of season brought a charge of witchcraft down on his head.

He was ahead of his time. The rediscovery of the classics during the Renaissance sparked a renaissance in composting, too. William Caxton, the first English printer, used his press to recommend "dungying and compostying the feldes." Shakespeare appreciated the powers of compost: "Do not spread compost on the weeds," Hamlet warns his mother. Robert Herrick, the seventeenth-century lyric poet, put the matter in perspective:

> The best compost for lands
> Is the wise master's feet and hands.

"Turn the clod and wheel thy compost home," advised William Cowper, the aristocratic poet who balanced his flights of fancy with manual labor in the garden.

Composting was a universal activity in Merry Olde England. Garbage disposal in those happy, spontaneous times was limited to heaving the stuff out the window; so that it all ended up together in that *de facto* composting bin, the gutter. In London, at least, the finished product was "as black as thick ink," according to Signor Busoni, the chaplain to the Venetian ambassador. The goo was eagerly sought by market gardeners, the Venetian noted in a report he made in 1618 to his employers. The gardeners used the compost to enrich their plots at the edge of the city, growing artichokes there that impressed even an old-country Italian.

The court of Louis XIV was no slouch in the composting department either. To supply all those wild balls and banquets, Louis needed produce year-round. For this he depended on "hot beds" filled with composting horse manure—these worked in the same way as the emperor Tiberius' cucumber patch. When fresh manure wasn't available in quantity (and not everyone could command the resources of a royal stable), gardeners stretched it with all sorts of substitutes. An English recipe of the period calls for "some horse litter already cold; straw steeped in pond water two or three days; grass; coal ashes and if they can be had, the grains of malt after brewing or damaged bran made very wet: if they are thrown together in a heap and well-watered with ferment and heat as well as any dung can desire."

As a nation of gardeners, the English were finding that their need for compost was growing much faster than the supply of animal manures in general. As a result, they became extraordinarily resourceful composters. A sampling of what went into an eighteenth-century compost heap might include, among other things, herring, blubber, hair, woolen rags, feathers, and furriers' clippings, the offals of the tannery or the glue factory, and the dung of seabirds, pigeon dung, and excrements of dogs and rabbits. No wonder they were ordering so many vegetables from France!

Colonists across the Atlantic didn't admire the mother country's politics, but they watched the English farmer's experiments with keen attention. Nearly all our founding fathers took a hand in this, even those who never set their hand to a plow. Benjamin Franklin, for example, put away his kite and key to experiment with soil improvement. He sowed powdered gypsum (then called "land plaster") on a hillside in Washington, spelling out in large letters that became ever more visible as the fertilized strips grew greener than the crops around them, "THIS FIELD HAS BEEN PLASTERED." Probably most of the farm workers were as well, which may be why Ben never advanced to composting.

With independence, composting developed presidential aspirations in America. George Washington was not only the father of our country, but one of the fathers of composting as well. According to one of his biographers, our first president "saved manure as if it were gold." He also left us records of a test he made comparing the compostability of various manures and soils.

Thomas Jefferson kept a farm book in which he outlined the records of his own composting experiments. James Madison added that "continual cropping without manure deprives the soil of its fertility."

The real empowerment of composting came with the writings of John Taylor, a Virginian who saw composting as an essential bulwark against Alexander Hamilton and those other Yankee bankers. In a series of letters to the newspaper, Taylor bemoaned the decline of American agriculture, a trend he saw was weakening the farmers' hold on government. He planned to restore both the soil and the political health of the country through a return to primitive virtue—a sort of crude composting system in which cattle or sheep were kept in a mobile pen. This enclosure was moved from spot to spot around the fields so that its inhabitants might heap each part with compost in turn. Awkward as this may seem, it was advanced thinking at a time when most Americans believed that plants derived their nutrients from the air—atmospheric manure, so to speak.

News of more sophisticated composting methods arrived in the United States with William Cobbett, a British journalist who was probably the only one of his trade to literally rake muck—journalism may have been his calling, but it was through farming that he earned his living. Cobbett made prolonged visits to America whenever his opposition to hallowed English customs such as public flogging seemed likely to land him in jail. Cobbett was as free with his opinions here as at home; he detested American democracy and wrote a book criticizing the quality of vegetable gardening in the United States.

"A man's morality," he wrote, "may be judged by the appearance of his garden. If that be neglected, he is nine out of ten times a sluggard, a drunkard or both."

Among the diatribes that fill *The American Gardener* are some remarkably sensible tips on building a compost heap. Cobbett maintained (correctly) that manure by itself is not a good fertilizer for vegetables; because it is too rich in nitrogen, it encourages rank, flavorless growth. "A great deal more is done by fermentation of manures than people commonly imagine," Cobbett advised, and he recommended composting the dung with leaves, weeds, and ashes or powdered shells (both sources of calcium, like the lime that most composters add to their heaps today). Cobbett also advised turning the heap to spread decomposition—all in all, his gardening seems to have been much sounder than his politics.

It was New Englanders, though, who really took composting to heart; anything that could transform refuse into profit was sure to appeal to those thrifty souls. Fish, which was then to be harvested cheaply and easily from the coastal waters, was a favorite material for composting in this region of the country. After all, New Englanders had been baiting their fields with this stuff ever since Squanto the Indian taught the Pilgrims to plant a fish in each hill of corn.

Typically, Connecticut Yankees figured out that through composting they could turn this source of fertility into a salable dry fertilizer, and hence a source of profit. In their hands, fish composting became a substantial business. By the middle of the last century, one fertilizer manufacturer in New Canaan, Connecticut, processed 220,000 fish in this way over a single season.

The dangers of this emerge from a Vermonter's (Thomas G. Fessenden) manual of rural living, *The Husbandman and Housewife,* published in Bellows Falls in 1820. Besides offering the first nonsexist guide to composting, this also documented one of the first great composting failures: "Mr. Young records an experiment in which herrings were spread over a field ploughed in for wheat and produced so rank a crop that it was entirely laid before harvest." Our guess is that the crop was rank in more ways than one. Incidentally, Fessenden also gave instructions for composting any large mammals that might wander into and expire in your vegetable garden. Casualty rates for the neighbors were not indicated.

Meanwhile, back in the old country, an industrious German named Baron Justus von Liebig was sowing the seeds for the artificial fertilizer industry. "If I could procure," he wrote in 1840, "elsewhere the substances which gave manure their value in agriculture, we should not need the latter." This was no casual boast, either, for von Liebig was a brilliant chemist, and had no trouble in putting his finger on the exact chemicals he needed. To supply phosphorus, for example, he simply treated old bones with sulfuric acid, to produce that super-rich fertilizer we now call "superphosphate." Von Liebig succeeded in creating a whole new industry—but at the same time he disrupted the age-old rhythm of recycling materials back into the earth.

In truth, though, it is unfair to blame von Liebig for what followed, for the German chemist also insisted on the importance of recycling all nutrients from human refuse to the land. He found particularly shocking London's modern sewer system, which flushed all the sewage out to sea. What offended von Liebig the most was the fact that England had so enthusiastically adopted his method of fertilizer manufacture.

Von Liebig thundered,

> England is robbing all other countries of the sources of their fertility. In her eagerness for bones, she has turned up the battlefields of Leipzig, of Waterloo, and of the Crimea; already from the catacombs of Sicily she has carried away the skeletons of generations. Annually her ships remove from other countries the manurial equivalent of three millions and a half of men. She takes from us the means of supporting, and squanders it down her sewers to the sea. Like a vampire she hangs around the neck of Europe—nay, of the entire world! And sucks the heart blood from nations without a thought of justice toward them and without a shadow of lasting advantage to herself.

The British didn't listen, but an upstate New York farm boy did. His name was Samuel W. Johnson, and he had a degree from Yale by the time he went to study chemistry with von Liebig. Johnson was a chemist through and through. After two years in Europe, he returned to his alma mater to take a research position in its new laboratory and he made his reputation through chemical analyses of fertilizers, exposing the quacks in what was by now a booming industry. Yet though he spent most of his adult life with test tubes and retorts, Johnson never forgot the lessons of his childhood, and he retained a great fondness for muck.

In the *Essays on Peat, Muck, and Commercial Manures* that he published in 1859, Johnson strongly urged on farmers the use of swamp muck. Dredge the organic rich slop out of every swamp (ever wonder how we lost our wetlands?) and spread it right over the fields, he advised. Or better yet, mix it with horse manure (two parts muck to one part horse apples) and compost it.

Like every great composter, Johnson was an opportunist, and he'd pop anything handy into the heap: scraps from the slaughterhouse or soap boiler, even waste from the glue factory. So strongly did Johnson believe in the value of composting that he wanted his own testimonial painted—"in bold letters"—on every barn door in Connecticut. Later, as director of the nation's first agricultural experiment station (located in New Haven) Johnson didn't need to go knocking on doors. The farmers came to him, and they got lectures on composting.

Unfortunately, what many of the farmers preferred was the advertisements of the fertilizer manufacturers—they promised immediate and miraculous results for just a few dollars down. Who could resist? Yet within two years of the publication of Johnson's book, the whole country was very forcibly reminded of what could happen when you didn't return organic matter to the soil.

The reminder was the Civil War. There were, of course, many reasons for this conflict, but destructive agricultural practices were a major factor in pushing North and South into a confrontation. Despite all the lectures from our founding fathers, few southern farmers made much effort to return anything to the soil.

New Englanders, at least the more enlightened individuals of that region, might be hauling muck compost out to their fields, but they had an economic interest in preserving the soil. They owned what they tilled. Slaves and overseers, those who actually did the farming in the South, did not. Besides, northern farms were, typically, small since they generally included only as much land as an extended family could work. In addition, the northern climate is more conducive to the preservation of humus, so that a manageable amount of compost had an impact.

A southern planter, by contrast, might own dozens of slaves and had to keep them all profitably employed—that required hundreds and thousands of acres. The southern soils (as Tom discovered during a four-year sojourn in Texas) can devour endless quantities of organic matter, so that to provide enough for a whole cotton or tobacco plantation would have been a gargantuan task. Anyway, to do so would have cut into the profits that supported the owner's aristocratic lifestyle. What the planters preferred to do was to exhaust the land and move on to a new tract of virgin land, generally on the frontier.

That's why a continuation of slavery in the Old South wasn't enough. Planters needed the new land out west, and when the Yankees resisted letting them take their slaves there, the planters knew their way of life was threatened. So in 1861 they seceded.[1]

Compost consciousness was still in its infancy, and no statesman on either side—North or South—made composting a part of his peace program. But a nurse in

---

[1]For an in-depth exploration of this subject, see William Chandler Bagley, Jr., *Soil Exhaustion and the Civil War* (Washington, DC: American Council on Public Affairs, 1942).

Washington, named Walt Whitman, did. "Behold this compost!" he wrote. "Behold it well." The material he recommended in his poem of that title—*This Compost*—was timely, though grim: he was marveling at the composting that comes, sooner or later (and during the Civil War much sooner) to every human body. Still, even if we can't recommend Walt's recipe, we appreciate the sentiment. In his search for a truly American poetic voice, he had hit on what should have been a truly American prescription for healthy soil. It *was* the prescription of one freed slave: George Washington Carver. A compost heap, he knew, a heap well made according to the instructions in his extension manuals, could be a means to self-sufficiency for the poor African-American smallholders of the South.

In the end, neither Johnson nor Whitman or Carver, nor any of their disciples, proved a match for U.S. industry. It was producing wastes—wastes of a new and far more toxic kind—and it had to dispose of them. If they could *sell* the wastes, so much the better. A ferocious competition was the keynote of that age of the robber baron; the dollars you squeezed out of by-products might be the only profits you would make in a battle with a Rockefeller or Carnegie. Who knew or cared about the cost to the environment?

So the Carnegies and Fricks figured out how to extract phosphorus from the slag that piled up around their steel mills. And the coal gas producers, those folks who piped in light to your home or school, they figured out how to extract nitrates from their wastes. What were the meatpackers going to do with those rivers of blood that poured out of their stockyards, those mountains of hooves and horns and bones? Sell them back to the farmers, and make back some of the money they had paid for the hogs and cattle in the first place. No one understood packaging better than the meat packers—

the country was shocked when Sinclair Lewis told it what was *really* in those sausages. Maybe the farmers would have been shocked if they knew the truth about the fertilizers that were impoverishing their soil—even in the meat packers' "organic" fertilizers, there was no humus—at the same time as they were bringing in bumper crops.

The great supplier of fertilizers today is the natural gas industry—it takes 20 cubic feet of their fossil fuel to produce a single pound of nitrate for the farm, lawn, or garden. In truth, though, it's not fair to point the finger at any one industry, since the real problem has been humanity's fondness for the quick fix. We can't resist the spectacular results a heavy dose of fertilizer will bring, and we've been willing to let the future take care of itself.

In 1900, over 90 percent of fertilizers came from natural sources; half a century later the figure had declined to 1 percent, and today virtually all fertilizers are manmade. In India and other parts of the undeveloped world, organic fertilizers still represent a larger proportion of those used, but if present trends continue it's just a question of time before artificial fertilizers come to dominate those cultures as well.

What's the problem with that? There's nothing wrong with artificial fertilizers *per se.* They are useful as a nutritional supplement; they are harmful only when we use them as a substitute for better stewardship of the soil. Albert Howard, the founder of the organic farming movement, and the man who is regarded as the father of modern composting, pointed out over fifty years ago how seductive artificial fertilizers are. He pointed out how the availability of cheap synthetic fertilizers had distracted our attention from recycling the organic wastes that we already have readily available. Even when Howard was writing, the era in which it was easier to move than conserve was passing. Today the virgin lands are gone, and we must take better care of what we have left.

Thus it's not difficult to see why in recent years there has been such a spectacular growth in composting. It's our fervent hope and belief that this represents a return to a kind of agricultural and general cultural sanity. In the next chapters, we'll show just how easy it is to return your little corner of the world to this time-honored tradition.

CHAPTER 3

How to Save the World While You Save Time and Money

TWO SNAPSHOTS:

1. Fresh Kills Landfill, a 2,400-acre mountain of garbage squatting at the southwestern edge of New York City. A disheveled counterpoint to the crystal towers up across the harbor in Manhattan, and in its own way equally impressive—the mound of refuse and rats is turning into the highest peak on our Atlantic Coast south of Maine.

2. A field in Tennessee. Or maybe it would be more accurate to call this the *ghost* of a field. Wind and rain have swept away the topsoil, peeling off layer after layer of earth until the surviving trees stand on earthen pedestals more than ten feet high.

What do these two scenes have in common? More than you might think. To some extent, they are the opposing sides of a single equation. Understand this, attack it in the right way, and we may just manage to resolve the two crucial problems simultaneously.

That's not to suggest that the remedy will be simple, nor that we (Marty and Tom) have *the* answer. But we are confident that composting will be a key to any solution. We are sure of this because we know that organic matter is a common denominator in both our waste disposal crisis and soil loss. Both represent a problem with our "solid waste stream" (as sanitary engineers like to call it—"garbage" sounds so unsanitary). There are all sorts of reasons the field eroded. These range from rural poverty to local topography, but any explanation must include this fact—that the supply of organic waste deposited there has been too little. At Fresh Kills, clearly there has been too much.

So why don't we take from one and give to the other? That's where composting enters the picture.

But maybe you don't think you have a problem with waste disposal. Put the stuff out on the curb, the garbage crew picks it up, and it disappears. Fresh Kills is an aberration, just like the rest of New York City.

Wrong. Practically every state in the nation has more garbage now than it knows what to do with, and in nearly every urban or suburban area solid waste is turning into a tsunami that threatens to drown us all.

In 1990, according to the Environmental Protection Agency (EPA), the last year for which it has assembled statistics, the United States generated 195 million tons of solid waste. That may seem appalling but actually it's a very conservative estimate; *Biocycle,* an independent journal of the solid waste industry, set the figure (for 1991) at 281 million tons. For the sake of argument, though, let's accept the EPA's figure. That's still more than twice as much garbage as we produced thirty years ago. In other words, our garbage production has increased 100 percent while the population increased by just 25 percent. Get out your calculator and you will discover that 195 million tons translates into 4.3 pounds of garbage *daily* from every American man, woman, and child.

How to visualize that amount of garbage . . .

Consider: if we tried to cart away a year's worth all at once, we'd need a caravan of 10-ton trucks long enough to reach more than halfway to the moon. Or take the cradle-to-grave perspective—you personally will discard 20,301 beer bottles, 10,370 aluminum cans, and 48,715 pounds of paper products in your lifetime.

Undoubtedly, our garbage will rank as our greatest national accomplishment. The Great American Novel, a jazz riff, a rock-and-roll ballad, or a tap dancing solo, whatever your personal contribution to civilization may be, it pales beside our collective accomplishment as waste generators. Don't believe us? Then listen: already that rubbish mountain in New York has outgrown the Great Wall of China to become the most massive man-made structure. To monitor conditions and help with the design, the city has retained a staff of geologists—management fears not only toxic leakage but also avalanches and cave-ins. "No one has ever attempted anything like this before," the city's sanitation commissioner explains, "so naturally we worry."

The Romans built roads and aqueducts, the Egyptians built pyramids, but we Americans overshadow them all with our dumps.

So we'll recycle.

Certainly we will. We are already doing that, collecting waste paper, cans, and bottles in an impressive total of 3,955 different programs nationwide. More and more communities are lining the curb with colorful plastic tubs — and the result is a 14-percent reduction in the flow to the landfill. Government planners hope they can increase that to 25 percent—but even if we do that while also holding trash production to the present level (and that seems unlikely), we will still have 146 million tons of garbage to deal with every year.

So we'll burn it in trash-to-energy plants.

We are already doing that too. Currently we burn approximately 10 percent of the garbage we produce, thereby generating some 0.11 quads of electrical and steam power a year (an amount equal to the energy of 52,000 barrels of oil each day). The EPA wants to increase this type of garbage disposal as well, so that it also handles about 25 percent of the stream. It seems like a great solution: get rid of something you don't want to produce something that you need.

195 Million Tons of Trash Generated Yearly

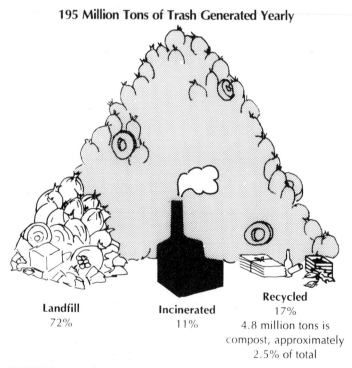

| Landfill 72% | Incinerated 11% | Recycled 17% 4.8 million tons is compost, approximately 2.5% of total |

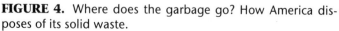

FIGURE 4. Where does the garbage go? How America disposes of its solid waste.

Why then are all those people fighting against the location of incinerators in their communities?

Unfortunately, there *are* problems with incineration. The older type of plant, the omnivores that handle two-thirds of the garbage disposed of in this manner, are dirty. They burn everything that comes out of your can, all in the same firebox. Some of that unsorted trash burns clean, but a lot doesn't, and the random mix of fuels keeps the temperature of the burn low so that more waste survives.[1] In the ash that such mass-burn incinerators sift down over the surrounding landscape there is generally an unhealthy dose of toxins: heavy metals such as cadmium and mercury (both deadly and persistent poisons) as well as arsenic and dioxin. In addition, the ash that remains inside the incinerator must often be handled as hazardous waste, which means that it must be kept isolated and contained, away from any place where it can seep down to poison the groundwater.[2]

The new generation of incinerators is equipped with scrubbers, filters, and precipitators that draw most of the ash out of the exhaust before it is released into the atmosphere. Their output may still be considerable; a study of a state-of-the-art facility on Cape Cod found

---

[1] Ironically, this is an environmental problem that is exacerbated by recycling and composting. By reducing the fraction of paper in the waste stream, recycling programs degrade its fuel value; and programs to divert yard waste (which consists largely of wood) degrades it further, so that in ecologically minded communities a ton of garbage contains far fewer BTUs than it did a decade ago.

[2] This has been the subject of litigation recently. The federal government has decided to exempt the incinerator ash from regulation, reasoning that because *household waste* is exempt then the ash produced by burning this waste should be exempt too. Some local courts, however, have recognized the flawed logic of this argument and have taken steps to protect their areas of jurisdiction. It may be some time before this argument is resolved.

that it pumps 2,000 tons of poisonous chemicals, including 590 pounds of mercury and a ton of lead, out the stack every year. Besides, even those toxins that don't escape into the air do not disappear. They end up in the fly ash—which ends up being even more toxic than that of the old-fashioned omnivore incinerators.

State-of-the-art incinerators aren't cheap, either—they cost $300 million or so apiece. Nor do they eliminate a community's solid waste problem. Incineration may reduce the volume of the waste by 90 percent, but the ash it produces still ends up in the same place—the landfill.

So what about landfills? They are still the standby: 76 percent of our garbage goes directly to the dump. How much longer that can continue, though, is anybody's guess, because the American landfill is almost as close to extinction as a spotted owl. Two-thirds of all landfills in the United States have closed since 1970–1,000 closed in 1990 alone, another 514 in 1991. That left a total of just 5,812 to serve the whole country. As best as the experts can figure, a third of those remaining will close by 1995, and in fifteen more years a total of perhaps 1,200 will remain. Nor will there be many new landfills opening up to replace the old ones.

Finding a site where large-scale dumping won't imperil the water supply is difficult enough, and where such sites do exist local residents almost always fight the creation of a new Fresh Kills. At the present rate of dumping, many states, including several of the most populous, look forward to exhausting *all* their existing landfills within a few years. Massachusetts and Connecticut, for example, will have filled theirs by 1997, while New York, Wisconsin, and Michigan will follow suit by 2002.[3] Even the uniquely endowed state of Texas

---

[3] "The State of Garbage in America," *Biocycle,* April 1992, p. 48.

(there are 750 dumps presently in operation there) should be filled to capacity by the year 2004. Nationwide, there's an average life of 12.5 years left to our landfills. What each state does after the gates to its last landfill close forever will vary with its circumstances, naturally. One thing is certain, though: any alternative means of disposal will cost it far, far more.

The fact is, taking out the garbage has become a terrifying budget-buster. Alabama, for example, a relatively poor state (it ranks forty-first in per capita personal income), is one that will probably close its last existing landfill by 1997. Of the 4.5 million tons of solid waste its residents generate each year, Alabama disposes of 89 percent through landfilling at an average cost of $10 per ton; switching to incineration could increase annual costs by $40 million, if the expense of that process doesn't rise above a very modest $20 per ton.[4]

On a more humble level, Tom's hometown of Middletown, Connecticut—a community of 42,000—paid $992,594 for trash collection last year. The biggest single item in that budget was tipping fees—the state-managed "resource recovery plant" charges Tom and his neighbors $56 for each ton of garbage they unload there. That's a major reason why Tom composts.

He knows that a huge proportion of his garbage is compostable and so need never be removed from the yard. As a fairly typical suburban householder, more than a quarter of his garbage consists of food and yard wastes—hedge trimmings, leaves, and grass clippings. The recycling consultant at City Hall told him that yard wastes constitute 18 percent of Middletown's waste

---

[4] *Biocycle* magazine's annual survey, "The State of Garbage in America" (April 1992, p. 48), reported tipping fees at incinerators as ranging from a low of $12 per ton in Montana to $40 in Florida and Iowa, $55 in Massachusetts, and $83 in Minnesota.

stream, while food wastes add another 8 percent.[5] There's no need for the city to truck this resource 15 miles away to that incinerator on the outskirts of the state capital before recovering it—that is best done in the row of composters at the back of Tom's yard. Those devices are not only crucial to the success of Tom's to-mato plants, they work hard to contain his tax rate.

Think we're giving those composters too much credit? Ask the mayor of Oyster Bay, Long Island. By the mid 1980s, no landfill in his county, state, or even geo-graphical region would accept his community's garbage at a price he could afford. He was willing to spend plenty, too. He was paying $115 to $138 *per ton* to truck the town's garbage out to Athens County, Ohio.[6] And in autumn, half of each truckload was bags of leaves.

Since 1989, though, the leaves at least have stayed at home, returned each year to Oyster Bay's residents as 11,000 tons of free compost. Although establishing a

---

[5]Obviously, these figures vary with the community; on p. 28 of *The Biocycle Guide to Yard Waste Composting* (Emmaus, PA: JG Press, 1989) I found the information that if I lived in Columbia, South Carolina, yard waste would make up fully 40 percent of my trash. To some de-gree, the composition of your trash is regional: residents of inner cit-ies don't discard any yard wastes, and Arizonans don't face the same leaf problems as New Englanders. But nationwide, the average can's-worth of garbage includes 19.9 percent yard waste and 8.5 percent food waste, as well as 34 percent of another compostable, paper.

[6]Garbage has become one of New York State's largest exports. To-gether with its neighbor New Jersey, it supplies more than 50 percent of all the tonnage shipped between one state and another. But they are far from alone in this practice. All but twelve states export at least some of their solid waste to cheaper landfills in other states—and most of the exporters also accept garbage from even more desperate neighbors. Indiana, which has complained publicly about the trash being sent there from New Jersey, meanwhile sends some of its load to Ohio; and Missouri, while sending 34 percent of its trash out of state, takes in the garbage from four others. This is one aspect of life in the global village that Marshall McLuhan never foresaw.

leaf-composting center involved the hiring of new staff and the purchase of trucks, shredders, and other equipment to collect, mix, and turn the compost, still the town determined that it would be cheaper to return the leaves to the soil as organic matter rather than export them out of state. Those savings may be considerable, too. Bowling Green, Kentucky, no longer talks of fall cleanup — officials in that city of 50,000 speak of the "leaf harvest."

It's quite a crop — half a million cubic feet of leaves every fall. Homeowners used to bag these and send them off to the landfill like everyone else, until a couple of agriculturalists at the state university there decided that urban leaves might be a resource for farmers. As part of a research project, they convinced homeowners to stop bagging their personal harvests, and to rake them to the curb instead, where municipal trucks could vacuum them up.

The trucks haul the crop to the university farm, where the leaves are ground in a tub grinder — the type of machine farmers use to shred hay bales — and the brown confetti that results is piled in windrows 8 to 10 feet high and 20 feet wide. Every few weeks, a front-end loader turns the windrows to aerate the leaves, and in about six months they reduce themselves to a fine, mature compost. This sells to landscapers for $5 per cubic yard, with the result that Bowling Green now pays $200,000 less for the annual leaf disposal.

That's chump change, too, compared to savings other communities are realizing. Islip, New York, for example, calculates that it saves $5 million each year just by composting grass clippings. The town used to export 20,000 tons of these every year.[7] Seattle is in the process

---

[7] Islip was also the community that sent a garbage-filled barge — the *Mobro 4000* — on a 6,000-mile journey. After a two-month trip that

of distributing some 70,000 compost bins to residents, and has already invested $5 million in this program. It looks like a very smart investment, too. For each ton of yard or food waste converted to humus in some backyard, the city saves $20; and the city calculates that 40 percent of all residential garbage could be treated this way.

Such a painless means of cutting the budget economy should be irresistible in these hard times, and it is. Yard waste composting is a can't-lose political cause, one that has had the governor of Georgia wearing a "Compost Man" T-shirt and that is mandated by state law now in sixteen states. As of the beginning of 1992, there were 2,201 yard waste composting operations up and running in the United States. What's more, yard waste composting is only a beginning. The more enthusiastic advocates of community-wide composting programs calculate that more than 60 percent of all municipal solid waste is compostable. Critics point out that much of that is recyclable paper, which is better sent to the mills than to the compost heap, but even they would agree to a figure of almost a third.

So far, achieving a consensus on what portion of our trash should be composted has proved impossible—no one even seems to agree on exactly how much trash there is out there. But suppose we accept the figures put forward by the Composting Council, a trade group formed to promote this process. It estimates that our towns should be recycling 80 million tons of waste in this fashion every year. How much money could that shave off of municipal budgets?

---

took it down into the Caribbean, the barge returned home, cargo intact. How many Islip taxpayers could afford the vacation that their garbage got?

It's hard to assign a typical cost for landfilling waste over the whole of the United States, since local costs may vary from $8 per ton in remote, rural Idaho to over $100 in a densely populated portion of the Northeast. It's worth noting, though, that the areas that produce the most garbage are those which, because of their population density, cannot practically increase their landfill capacity. Not surprisingly, those same areas have been and will be the leaders in municipal solid waste composting. Let's say, though, again for the sake of argument, that the average savings for each ton of waste composted equals Seattle's estimate of $20. So countrywide composting could save us $1.6 billion every year. That's not going to erase the federal budget deficit, but it's a lot of money even by Washington standards.

We should note at this point that environmentalists have some legitimate concerns about the composting of municipal solid waste. They point out that as handled today, solid waste is a very mixed bag. Among the innocent potato peelings, you find glossy brochures printed with lead and dioxin, polishes and cleansers full of toxic solvents, and quite likely some of those burnt-out AA batteries that you are supposed to return to the store for proper disposal, but just didn't—those may be laced with zinc, cadmium, lead, or other heavy metal toxins. Opponents of wholesale composting fear that the product turned out at municipal plants will be so tainted as to be of dubious value.

That is exactly what has happened in some cases. Industry studies have found that compost produced from unsorted garbage ("mixed" waste) contains five to *fifty* times as much lead, and as much as twenty-eight times as much cadmium, as compost from source-separated garbage (garbage that the homeowner has sorted into compostable and uncompostable fractions).[8] Fortunately, the indiscriminate, toss-it-all-in-together composters are in the minority, but the fact that they are allowed to operate at all has turned many environmentalists against solid waste composting.

It has also stunted the development of markets. After all, what farmer is going to "improve" his fields with a compost that may make them unfit for the cultivation of food crops?[9] At the time of this writing, twenty-one facilities are composting municipal solid waste in the United States, and some sixty more are planned or already under construction. But although the existing plants collectively process 2,000 tons of garbage each day, the overwhelming bulk of their output still goes to landfills. So far, composting is serving mainly as a less controversial form of incineration. It reduces the bulk of the waste by 50 percent or more and weight by about a third,[10] and "composting" *sounds* much healthier, so it's easier to sell to the community.

There are practical solutions to this problem of contamination, solutions that have proven successful in a number of community composting programs — we'll deal with these in detail in Chapter 9. The fact is, we have no choice but to resolve this situation. In 1992, a nationwide survey of "solid waste management pro-

---

[8] Figures taken from a study reported by Bernd Franke in *Biocycle* 33, no. 8 (July 1987). For a more complete treatment of this problem see Chapter 9, pages 206–214.

[9] This is precisely what has happened in the Netherlands, where farmers who have accepted composted mixed waste find that their vegetables sell for a lower price than those of competitors whose fields are compost- and (presumably) heavy metal–free.

[10] The volume reduction is due chiefly to compaction; the weight lost is mostly that of water vapor and carbon dioxide gas, by-products of decomposition that escape into the atmosphere.

fessionals" found that 96 percent believe composting must increase. Fewer than 10 percent believe that incineration, landfilling, or other means of waste disposal will expand — and waste managers are confident that the waste stream will continue to swell. They know this output has to go somewhere. We won't have any choice but to compost.

Which means we will be doing the right thing, even if for the wrong reason. The fact is, our garbage is a fantastically valuable resource. We learned in the first Earth Day, back in 1970, that throwing away bottles and cans was extravagant as well as sloppy, but somehow we overlooked the humus that was going into the dump with them. That is the really essential kind of recycling. We can get along without aluminum or glass — but we can't survive without humus.

Remember that field in Tennessee?

Its desperate condition is, as we noted at the beginning of this chapter, the result of many factors. Nature is partly to blame, for soil erosion is a natural process. But it's a process that has been greatly accelerated by abusive human practices. We indulge in many of those, from clear-cut logging and Christmas tree farming to strip mining and above all by exploitive methods of farming. As a result, we Americans are losing 1.7 *billion* tons of topsoil to erosion every year. And the crucial distinction between the good topsoil we are losing and the degraded subsoil that remains is primarily the organic content.

Check the textbooks, call the Soil Conservation Service, and you will find that technically and legally, there is no distinction between topsoil and subsoil other than which one lies closer to the surface of the ground. We like to think of topsoil as dark, crumbly, rich stuff, but if you stood in the middle of the Sahara, the top layer of soil might be pure sand, and that would be topsoil there. Where our topsoil *is* better, that's because organic matter enters the soil through the top: nature deposits dead vegetation and animal waste mainly at the surface.

Typically, the organic content of the soil is quite small. A rich prairie soil probably contains no more than 5–6 percent organic matter, while the soil of a southwestern desert may contain as little as 0.1 percent. Yet this tiny fraction brings the soil to life.

It's the organic matter—the humus—that glues the particles of silt, clay, and sand together in crumbs. That's what gives a healthy soil its structure, making it able to absorb and retain water, and guaranteeing that there will be enough air in the mix that plant roots can penetrate and survive. We noted in Chapter 1 that organic matter contributes most of a soil's fertility, and we'll detail in Chapter 4 how it helps the soil absorb and retain fertilizers. In discussing soil erosion, though, the most important fact is the obvious one that large crumbs of soil are far more resistant to displacement by either wind or water than the fine rock particles of which they are composed.

So humus is not only the heart of a good soil, it's also a principal defense against its loss. Indeed, one leading expert on erosion, R. P. C. Morgan of Britain's National College of Agricultural Engineering, uses a soil's organic content as a primary criterion for judging a soil's erodability—and a classic study by the Texas Agricultural Experimental Station[11] concluded that when organic content drops below 2 percent, that soil is at

[11] R. M. Smith, R. C. Henderson, and O. J. Tippit, *Summary of Soil and Water Conservation Research from the Blackland Experiment Station, Temple, Texas,* Bulletin No. 781 (College Station, TX: Texas Agricultural Experimental Station, 1954).

risk. In another study, conducted in Ghana, soil erosion in a sloping corn field was reduced by a spectacular 700 percent (from 3.64 metric tons per hectare to 0.52 metric tons) simply by digging in wood shavings at a rate of 5 tons per hectare.[12]

Yet in our exploitation of the soil Americans never calculate the value of the humus—what strip miner, logger, or farmer even, subtracts the value of the humus lost from the value of the harvest? Nor do we recognize the value of humus when we address the problems of soil loss. Our principal means of erosion control are mechanical. We treat the soil as something inert, something to be protected by wrapping it up with mulch or a cover crop, or by terracing or contour plowing. Then we string it along with a maintenance program of chemicals. What we need to do is not maintain; we need to rebuild. That's going to require all the solid waste we can get our hands on.

A few very practical people are already treating garbage as a natural resource. Municipal governments may be working on ways to reduce the waste stream, but the Composting Council recently published a report[13] advising on ways to maximize its impact. Add sewage sludge to yard waste or municipal waste, and you can stretch it to produce an additional 3 million tons of compost annually. Tap the horticultural profession for their waste, and you can add 15 million more tons to the pile. American farmers scrape some 180 million tons of manure from the barn, feed lot, and hen house

[12]M. Bonsu, "Organic Residues for Less Erosion and More Grain in Ghana," *Soil Erosion and Conservation* (Ankeny, IA: Soil Conservation Society of America, 1985), pp. 615–621.

[13]*Potential U.S. Applications for Compost* (Alexandria, VA: Solid Waste Composting Council, 1992).

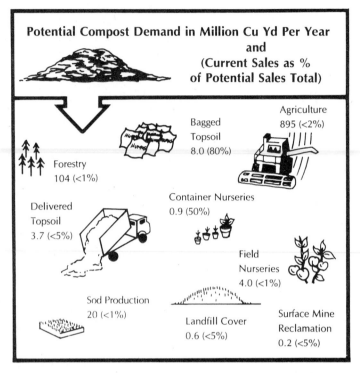

FIGURE 5. What could be, and what is: potential markets for compost in industry and the home, and the current sales, as percentage of potential totals (figures taken from the Composting Council's study, *Potential U.S. Applications for Compost*, Alexandria, Virginia, August 1992).

every year. Surely they could kick in yet another 3 million tons.

Altogether, the report calculates, we could and should be producing some 51 million tons of finished compost every year—102 million cubic yards. That's not nearly enough. This same report calculates the potential market at over a billion tons annually.

We could use 237 million cubic yards each year just in reclaiming stripped coal mines. Reforestation could absorb another 81 million cubic yards, and farming could take 895 million yards all by itself. It takes about 50 tons of compost, 100 cubic yards, to spread a ¾-inch-deep layer of organic matter over an acre of soil; that Tennessee farmer could use as much as 400 cubic yards to reclaim each acre of his or her lost field.

Do Marty and Tom really believe that every U.S. community is going to start composting? They don't see how we can afford not to. Quite apart from the cost of waste disposal, U.S. communities will tire of paying the costs of soil erosion. The mud that washes into streams and rivers (¼ billion tons a year into the Mississippi alone) is choking reservoirs, and the agricultural chemicals it brings with it are poisoning aquatic ecosystems. Mud has become the number one form of non–point-source pollution (pollution that cannot be traced back to a distinct source). The immediate cost is about $10 billion a year in damages to everything from fisheries to industrial cooling systems.

That's bad enough, but it's the future cost that's going to cripple us: we're destroying our ability to feed ourselves. Take Illinois as an example, and consider what one writer has called the "Great Terrain Robbery."[14]

For a century and a half, Illinois has been feeding a lot of Americans. This state habitually competes with Iowa for first place in corn and soybean production — and it does so because of its deep, prairie topsoil. When Anglo settlers arrived, this covered the state in a layer that averaged 9 inches deep. By the 1970s, this had thinned to 6 inches on average, and in many places had vanished altogether. Yet that was only a beginning. In

---

[14]James Krohe, Jr., "Illinois—The U.S. Bread-Basket," *The Ecologist*, vol. 14, nos. 5–6 (1984), pp. 189–193.

the 1970s, the United States developed a trade deficit, and the government decided to pay for all the VCRs and cars coming in by shipping out more agricultural commodities. Suddenly, Illinois was feeding the rest of the world, too.

With the inimitable Earl Butz as point man, the government urged farmers to put more land into production. "Plant fence row to fence row," he advised, meaning that they should cut down the windbreaks their grandfathers had planted and plow up the marginal lands they had never considered fit for cultivation. Crop rotation was abandoned in favor of continuous cropping with humus-consuming soybeans and corn. Not surprisingly, the soil's disappearing act speeded up, so that whereas erosion had reduced the fields' natural productivity by 2.2 percent over the whole previous century, by 1984 a study by the Illinois EPA found that productivity was dropping by 2 percent *each year.* A third of all our acreage is devoted to exports now, and what we are exporting, pretty clearly, is our topsoil.

So far we've been able to mask the damage with increased doses of fertilizers—we apply 58 percent more nitrates to our fields today than we did twenty years ago. Substituting synthetics for the nutrients that used to come from humus is expensive, of course, and in the long run it only worsens the problem. For as the humus level continues to decline, the soil retains less and less of the fertilizers we apply to it—we use more fertilizers and get less benefit from them. Anyway, while fertilizers can supply the nutrients plants require, they can't solve the other problems that humus depletion brings. For example, because a humus-deficient soil does not absorb or retain water well, any crop grown on it is far more vulnerable to drought.

Even the bureaucrats have had to agree that a crisis is in the making. Washington responded in 1985 and

again in 1990 with farm bills that mandated soil conservation measures for farmers who received federal
subsidies. Piling subsidies on top of subsidies, the federal government in 1985 began paying farmers to temporarily retire the marginal and erosion-prone land it
had urged into cultivation a decade before. Yet because
the drive for exports continues, the net effect has been
to actually increase the pressure on good agricultural
land.

The really constructive elements of these farm
bills—the low-input sustainable agriculture program
(LISA), for example—have received little more than lip
service as yet. LISA calls for the promotion of composting, but Congress has failed to fund it at more than
token levels. Composting hasn't got the kind of constituency that tobacco subsidies do. Not yet. But when
taxpayers start adding up the costs of waste disposal and
of soil erosion, that will change.

Indications are that most farmers would welcome
this change. Indeed, many are making it on their own.
An Agricultural Compost Association that formed in
April 1991 is already coordinating information among
800–1,000 members and is expanding from its original
base in the Northeast to regional chapters all over the
country. The association's goal is not only to promote
composting among farmers, but also to establish a market for their compost. Already a handful of farmers are
producing this as a new kind of crop.

They do this by charging local communities or industries for the disposal of nontoxic organic waste—
old telephone books, say, or raw scrap wool or spoiled
fruit and vegetables from supermarkets, and mixing
these with the manures produced by their own livestock. The disposal fees are one source of income, and
the sale of the finished compost to landscapers may be
another—unless farmers choose to use the compost on

their own fields, in which case it may reduce or virtually eliminate their fertilizer bill.

Repairing the damage we have done to our land is going to be an expensive process, however, and not one that farmers can pay for by themselves. If 10 to 20 cubic yards (5 to 10 tons) of compost are needed to protect each acre of cropland from erosion (and that is the Composting Council's estimate), how is a farmer going to buy or produce the 5,000 or so tons needed to treat a modest farm? We have benefited from foods priced artificially low; if we want to pay the bill we have run up in lost topsoil, we must start paying the true cost of a loaf of bread and subsidize healthy agricultural practices.

That's still in the future. The wonderful thing about composting, though, is that it's a revolution you can start on your own. Putting a bin in your own yard and encouraging your neighbor to do the same can have a significant impact on the solid waste flow (and tax dollar flow) of your town. For proof you need look no further than the garbage cans of Alameda County, California. When the state ordered it to cut its waste production in half by the end of the century, Alameda decided to begin with a home-composting education program. It has since found that people who attend one of its workshops (a couple of thousand to date) typically set about a can less garbage on the curb per week. That's a 25 percent reduction, ¼ ton less garbage per year, and a full half of the savings each resident must achieve.

A far more ambitious program is underway in Seattle, Washington. That city is distributing 70,000 compost bins to residents, while a volunteer group, Seattle Tilth, is providing "trainers" to help recipients assemble the bins and put them to work. Because each Seattle household produces, on average, 520 pounds of yard waste annually, full use of these bins could lighten the load the city must haul away by as much as 18,000 tons.

Seattle Tilth is more conservative in its projections, counting on the cooperation of one-third of the bin recipients—that seems reasonable, since by mid-1991 20 to 25 percent of the city's single-family households were in fact composting to some extent. Even that level of compliance will generate substantial savings—and could do so in your community, too. If one-third of Tom's neighbors in Middletown followed suit, and cut the community's annual waste production by, say, 2,800 tons, that would save the taxpayers there almost $160,000. And what price can you put on the other benefit—that every householder would leave a half- or quarter-acre scrap of the landscape healthier for the next generation?

Which brings us back to New York City and Fresh Kills. In the shadow of its four garbage peaks, there are compost piles now. The city of New York's financial crisis delayed funding for its recycling programs, and each of the five boroughs initially insisted on establishing its own incompatible system. But with funding back in place as of 1992, and the boroughs coming to terms, the city hopes to reduce trash by 42 percent by the year 2000. Once again, there is no alternative. Within a few years of that date, Fresh Kills is slated to close.[15] By then, the city should be producing up to 3.15 million cubic yards of compost a year.

City officials claim that they will be able to sell much of that to the private sector. Maybe. But what they are making now in a pilot project—3,100 tons processed from the leaves of Staten Island—stays mostly at

---

[15] Although the life span of this operation is lengthening as recycling takes hold in New York City. The irony is, as Bill Young pointed out, that the more environmentally minded the people of Staten Island prove, the longer they will have to live with an active landfill. With municipal composting coming on line now, Fresh Kills may not close for another twenty years.

the dump. Residents of Staten Island are allowed to take some compost home with them, and a few truckloads are distributed to community gardens, schools, and parks.

But Bill Young hates to see any of it leave.

He's the landscape architect who since the late 1980s has been working with the Department of Sanitation to turn the dump into a garden spot. Compare him to Frederick Law Olmsted (the creator of Central and Prospect parks, and the last designer to have a comparable stretch of New York landscape with which to work), and you make Bill terribly nervous. The people who impress him are the engineers like his chief, Phil Gleason, the people who are making the landfill work.

Yet as of January 1993, Bill had helped arrange the planting of some 52,000 trees and shrubs; and that, according to him, was just a small beginning. So far most of the planting has gone to the 18-foot-tall berm of earth the department piled around the landfill's perimeter to hide it from the surrounding community. Bill dismisses this as a standard device. What interests him is the planting that is beginning in the landfill's interior as each of its four peaks fills to capacity and the engineers cap it off (and two peaks are slated for closure by the end of 1993). That's where Bill needs the compost.

The cap begins with a gas-collecting membrane (methane from Fresh Kills heats 15,000 homes on Staten Island), or else an impermeable layer of compacted clay; then comes 24 inches of sandy subsoil, then 6 inches of what is, nominally, topsoil. But what gets delivered to Fresh Kills under that name doesn't satisfy Bill, and it needs a big dose of organic matter before it will support the native plant and animal communities he envisions.

Native prairie grasses and wildflowers—little bluestem and switch grass; asters, black-eyed Susans, and milkweeds—are the pioneers, for the Department of

Sanitation is planting them to stabilize the capping soil. This choice isn't a statement, it's common sense. The deep-rooted prairie plants bind the soil much more effectively than the lawn grasses that the department used formerly, and unlike the lawn grasses, the prairie plants thrive without irrigation. But they are accustomed to an organic-rich soil. And a healthy, lively soil is even more essential for what is going to come next.

You can get a glimpse of that in the six acres Bill Young and Phil Gleason have reclaimed at the landfill's northernmost tip. There they reshaped the earth from bulldozer flat to swells and hollows and planted an expanse of natural sand dune vegetation and the oak and pine scrub forest that would shelter it. Six acres is a small piece of the total 2,400, the creators admit, and when they have proven that the plants won't damage the landfill's cap, they hope to create many more such patches. But nature isn't waiting for them.

Already the island of trees and shrubs has attracted hawks and quail, snowy egrets and great blue herons, as well as a host of less spectacular fowl. These visitors, in turn, are eating and redepositing the seed, so that in the first year after landscaping, Young observed a spontaneous increase of one-third in the number of plants. This persuades him that there *will* come a day when the hawks and quail will finally displace the flocks of trash-picking gulls.

If this seems like a utopian dream, well, Fresh Kills has long been a visionary landscape. In the past, the dream was a bad one. But in the future, with the injection of a few million tons of compost, who knows?

The Uncrowned King

What do you do if you are Prince Edward Island and you've got 16,000 tons of diseased potatoes on your hands? Or if you're Taylor County, Florida, and the cost of landfilling crab shells and guts (3,000 tons a year) is eating up a quarter of your waste disposal budget? Or maybe you are just a private chicken farmer, and a fire has left you with 100,000 asphyxiated chickens and the state of Maine's Department of Environmental Protection is talking threats to the aquifer and fines that leave you breathless—what do you do?

You call Will Brinton.

He showed the provincial government how it could mix the potatoes with straw, hay, sawdust, and horse, cow, and pig manure into 15 miles of windrows—the biggest composting operation in the world—and "cook" the potatoes and their harmful virus too into a beneficial additive for the potato farmers' fields. The crab bits he mixed with four kinds of sawdust, wood chips and leaves, and dollops of chicken and cow manure to produce an odor-free compost that local residents fought to haul away (giveaway day caused a traffic jam). The chickens, an admixture of equal parts poultry manure and sawdust (2 gallons per chicken), reduced to humus within two months—all except the beaks.

A biodynamic farmer with a master's degree in soil and plant science, Brinton had wondered back in the early 1970s why two lots of what were ostensibly the same organic fertilizer or food often behaved so differently for him. To find out why, and provide sound scientific information for organic growers like himself, he joined with a chemist and founded Woods End Research Laboratory in 1974.

Soil testing tailored to the needs of organic growers was the initial service, but by 1980 Brinton was focusing on composting. Compost was his customers' main means of improving their soils, yet as Brinton recognized, the term was a loose one. Depending on the ingredients and the treatment, the product might indeed be a fine aid to soil fertility, but not infrequently the samples that came to Brinton were actually phyto-toxic—actively harmful to plant growth. To distinguish one from the other, Brinton began developing a set of chemical and physical tests for composts, tests that would provide objective data on quality and maturity. At the same time, he began investigating ways to predict how materials would behave in the heap, and methods for developing composting recipes.

When solid waste disposal became a national is-sue—around 1987 or 1988, as Will recalls—the former farmer found himself suddenly a star. Major corpora-tions all over the country wanted to try composting and Will (who had bought out his partner a couple of years previously) was the only person who could provide both theoretical expertise *and* practical knowledge. He was the alchemist who could change an organic waste into a "bioresource."

Often when these new clients contact Woods End about a material they want to compost, they don't even know exactly what they've got. Will's first job then is a complete analysis. The greasy, wet sludge from a gelatin manufacturer, for example, proves to be rich in nitro-gen; and though it's easier to put a name to the pigs that arrived from the lab of a pharmaceutical manufacturer, who has ever tried composting drug-laced pigs? After the analysis is complete, then Will and the staff go to work with their own computer modeling system to cre-ate a composting formula—which they use to run a small test batch in the laboratory.

Implementing the recipe is up to the client—Brin-ton does not manage the actual composting operations. He does commonly serve clients as a sort of middleman, however, putting the producers of complementary wastes in touch with each other. This matchmaking may link a fish-processing plant that wants to dispose of a thousand tons of dogfish "gurry" (a wet and nitrogen-rich bioresource) with a paper plant that has an excess of dry, carbon-rich wood fiber. Or the marriage may be between a cranberry packer (wet and carbonaceous fruits) and an egg producer (dry, nitrogenous manure) — their bioresources, when mixed with animal bedding from a research laboratory and waste paper, became the prime ingredients of the "Mass Natural Fertilizer" that a Massachusetts client is now marketing.

Brinton acknowledges that he was in the right place at the right time, but attributes his continuing success to foresight as well. He early recognized the next challenge that the new composters would face — what do you do with it once you've made it? How do you ensure that your compost is of good quality? Increasingly, he says, the lab workers are busy with quality assurance programs, testing the output of the composting operations they have designed. For this he uses a battery of chemical tests that determine not only its nutrient content but also factors such as CO_2 production (a clue to decomposer activity) that indicate chemical stability and maturity. Then, because this erstwhile farmer remains a practical man, he sows seed into a compost sample to see how the plants like it.

Woods End Research Laboratory preserves a homespun appearance. It's housed in an old horse barn set back in the forest outside Mount Vernon, Maine. But inside, on the wide board floors are banks of computers, flasks, an electronic composting simulator — and a photograph of Will consulting with fellow composter Prince Charles. Woods End maintains offices in Britain as well as Nova Scotia now, with a representative in the southern United States, too. Will commutes down to Orlando where he's advising Disney World on how to process its food and garden waste to enrich the park's sandy soil. Such a feasibility study typically costs $200,000 or more.

But if the lab's clientele is largely high-end now ("Fortune 50 Companies" is as specific as Will's discreet assistant would be), Will is in no one's pocket. When the Polish government flew him over to advise on what it could do to deal with the oceans of hog manure its agricultural industry produces (a source of water pollution), he reacted in a characteristically unexpected fashion to what he saw.

He admitted that the collectivized farms were appalling, places where no one took any pride in their work. But the 85 percent of the Polish farms — small private holdings — that never were collectivized, he found very impressive. Watching farmers carefully spread composted manure (as Americans used to do) and polish plowshares out in the field so that they would not carry a single crumb of soil away struck a responsive chord in the compost king. Perhaps, he suggests, these are the farmers who are going to show us the way to a sustainable harvest.[16]

State OKs Degradation in Prison System!

Money was clearly the motive for a New York State program as reported in the May 1991 issue of *Biocycle* magazine; the Department of Correction is saving $300,000 annually by composting food waste at twenty prisons. With kitchens there serving 134,000 meals every day, this system generates an impressive 217,000 tons of scraps and peelings every month—these used to go down the drain to the prisons' waste-water treatment facilities, or directly to the dump. Disposal had been cost-

---

[16]This last passage is paraphrased from Will Brinton's article — "Compost & Regeneration"—in the spring 1992 edition of *Orion Quarterly*, Vol. 11, No. 2, pp. 36–43.

ing approximately $625,000 a year, and in the fall of 1990 a report projected this would rise to $3.5 million by the year 2000. That's when the Department of Correction decided to take action.

Prison facility engineers cited the availability of inexpensive labor (an understatement—most inmates are paid $1.05 per day) as the reason for adopting a technologically unsophisticated, labor-intensive system of composting. Food scraps are mixed with wood chips made from the yard wastes of surrounding communities, and then heaped in windrows. Prisoners monitor the internal temperature of the composting materials with thermometers, turning the heaps as they cool with the aid of a front-end loader. As soon as degradation is completed, inmates spread the finished compost on the fields of prison farms.

In describing this operation, one Department of Correction official praised its rehabilitative value.[17] As proof, he cited inmates' competition for the job of "recycling porter"—the individual entrusted with collecting and sorting recyclables and compostables. Apparently these inmate workers are quite successful at ensuring full participation by fellows. "I have my ways of encouraging them to recycle," one such porter explained to the *Biocycle* reporter.[18]

Whatever the benefit to inmates, the composting *is* clearly succeeding as a rehabilitative program for prison soils. Which makes this program unique—enriching the fields while saving taxpayers millions runs counter to every basic law of state and federal agricultural policy.

---

[17] Robert Spencer, "Integrated Recycling Pays Off at Prison Facilities," *Biocycle,* May 1991, p. 49.
[18] Spencer, p. 48.

Regulation and Testing

Despite all the fine talk of billion-ton, million-dollar markets, composting has not as yet developed into a major industry. Nor will it, until the producers address the issue of consistency and quality control.

The fact is that not all commercial composts are created equal, and that what a consumer buys under this title can range from the very good to the truly toxic. We know of a nurseryman who lost $30,000 worth of container-grown perennials and shrubs because the compost he had bought to mix into potting soil was not sufficiently mature. The compost manufacturer had not waited until decomposition had finished before selling the product, so the compost robbed the potting soil of nutrients and the nurseryman ended up with a scrawny, unsalable crop. Needless to say, he won't be buying compost again soon.

There are at present no comprehensive, nationwide standards for compost. The Environmental Protection Agency (EPA) regulates compost made from sewage sludge, but its only concern is with toxicity to humans. The EPA standards govern the amount of heavy metals and pathogens the finished sewage sludge compost may contain, and assign uses to the product, ranging from landscaping to landfill coverage, according to the degree of contamination. Compost made from municipal solid waste falls under the supervision of the individual states, which are beginning to regulate for toxicity to humans.[19] None of these standards, however, addresses

---

[19]Currently, somewhat less than half the states have standards in place, but more and more are doing so. Typically the state regulations are based on the EPA sewage-sludge standards. For information about your state's compost standards, the reader can contact the state De-

the characteristics that are of importance to plants. This results in a most curious situation: as they shop for compost, farmers and landscapers commonly know whether they can eat with impunity what they buy, but they have no idea of the effect it will have on their crops.

What makes this situation particularly difficult is that the consumer cannot even rely on a producer's track record. As the situation now stands, a composting plant's profits are mostly in the tipping fees (the per-ton fee charged for accepting the waste) it collects (or if it's a municipally operated concern, in the tipping fees the plant eliminates). The result is that industrial composters generally take whatever wastes happen at the moment to be most abundant; they cannot afford to work to a recipe, so the product may vary drastically from day to day.

In addition, the wastes for which the composter can charge the highest tipping fees tend to be those with problems — that have a strong odor, say, or that are toxic to plants and water if spread directly onto the soil ("land farming" this is called). After all, the waste generator will pay most to get rid of something nobody wants to take. So economics encourage the production of poor-quality compost.

The obvious answer is establishment of industry-wide standards, but with "regulation" such a dirty word in Washington, the federal government has been unable or unwilling to show any initiative. Instead, leadership has come from individual states, counties, and municipalities — and of all the programs to certify compost quality, that of Portland, Oregon, has been the most impressive.

---

partment of Environmental Protection, or The Composting Council at 114 South Pitt Street, Alexandria VA 22314, tel. (703) 739-2401.

Portland is a major compost producer; it processes upward of 80 percent of all the residents' yard wastes, selling the resulting compost back to private citizens, as well as nurseries and landscapers. To ensure its market, the city tests its product periodically for a dozen different metals and arsenic, as well as a horrifying soup of chemical pesticides — and any detectable levels, incidentally, have been below those federal regulation allows in food. For the benefit of customers, the city also tests once every fiscal quarter for a variety of horticultural characteristics: the relative acidity of the compost (pH), its nutrient content, particle size, ability to retain water, the levels of soluble salts (which in excess may poison plant roots), and the presence of weed seeds. As the ultimate proof of the pudding, Portland even sows timothy grass seed in the compost samples to determine how hospitable the compost is to plant growth.

Portland's testing program provides most of the basic data customers need — with the sheet of test results, landscapers can determine if the municipal compost will suit their plantings. As such, it is an enormous step forward. But as a strictly regional effort, it's of limited value to an industry that to realize its potential must become interregional and interstate. The most serious limitation of the Portland system, though, is that it isn't user friendly. It forces the job of interpreting test results on the customers, who may not have the knowledge to do this. That, as the Composting Council recognizes, is not good business.

The formation of this trade association in 1990 was the result of corporate concerns — a number of giant manufacturers such as Procter & Gamble, Du Pont, and Kraft General Foods were experiencing not only big waste problems, but also growing problems with public image; they were being attacked (rightly or wrongly) as polluters and environmentally irresponsible. The council's original aim was to solve both problems by promoting recycling through composting—thus they could relabel waste packaging as an "organic resource," save money, and become environmental heroes all at the same time. And although the council now counts as members a number of universities and public agencies, it is regarded with some distrust by many composting activists, whose backgrounds tend to be in the counter-culture. In truth, the council's perspective continues in many ways to be corporate. That's proving to be its strength.

Because the council members think like business-people, they have begun asking a new kind of question: What does the *customer* need and want? As of late 1992, the council's marketing committee had identified sixty-five individual markets for compost and its standards committee was contacting the relevant professional associations to find out exactly what sort of compost was needed for each. With the help of the "Green Section"—the course superintendents' division—of the U.S. Golf Association, for example, council staffers have already written specifications for compost to be used in preparing the soil for golf course greens.

Like the Portland tests, these specifications will address safety issues (in general, the council plans to follow EPA guidelines) while also focusing on the physical and chemical characteristics that will determine a compost's horticultural performance. In addition, the council's specifications will include matters that determine sales appeal—the color and odor of the compost and the degree of contamination with man-made (albeit inert) substances such as plastic and glass.

The "specs" will vary with the market—athletic fields, for example, will need a more water-retentive compost than that which will serve the producers of potting soils for greenhouse crops. But the methodology used in each case will be the same. The same checklist of tests will be applied to all composts—and that will make it simple for producers to tailor their products to suit the needs of several different markets.

According to the council member charged with supervising this project, Philip Leege of Procter & Gamble, a complete set of specifications for all the identified markets won't emerge until 1995. But at that time he foresees the council registering compost producers, or perhaps providing some sort of symbol that they stamp on their products to show that they have met the minimum standards for a particular market. When that happens, customers will be able to buy compost with confidence that what they get will suit their needs. And then perhaps the billion-ton talk may become a reality.

CHAPTER 4

How to Save Money While You Save the World

I [TOM] AM FEELING EXTRAVAGANT; that's an unsettling feeling for a Yankee. But I *am* feeling extravagant, and so I'm going to dose the compost heap with cricket manure this afternoon.

Cricket manure's not cheap. But in partnership with the leaves, old sunflower stalks, and the vegetable parings I've already stacked in the bin, it will produce something that replaces a whole salesroomful of products at the garden center. Surely that's good economics.

The cricket manure comes to me from Georgia, and it costs $10.95 for a three-pound package. I can't recall ever having *paid* for manure before, and I've used wastes from animals far more exotic than crickets. When I was studying horticulture, I worked at a botanical garden right across the street from the Bronx Zoo. In those days, I had my choice of everything from elephant to penguin (aspergillosis-free ones), and it was mine by the truckload whenever I cared to come and pick it up. So it galls me now to pay for the stuff.

Although, actually, considering what you get with "Kricket Krap" (that's what the supplier calls it), the price isn't bad. To begin with, my three-pound bag holds about 1,425,000 droppings; that means they cost me less than 1/10,000 of a penny apiece. Each of those nuggets is, by weight, 4 percent nitrogen, 3 percent phosphorus, and 2 percent potassium; and those are the three major nutrients that every plant needs to grow.

True, I could get the same chemicals substantially cheaper in a synthetic form. A 10-pound sack of 5–10–5 sells for just $4.99 at the local garden center—I checked yesterday. A little math reveals that the chemist works for less than the cricket. But the synthetic may not have all the trace elements and minerals that a manure has, and plants need those things the way we need vitamins. Even more important from my point of view, the synthetic doesn't appeal to the bacteria in my compost heap. I've tried sprinkling 5–10–5 in my bin, and it hasn't had any perceptible effect on the progress of the composting.

Presumably the microorganisms in the heap do consume the fertilizer, because the granules disappear by the time the compost is finished. But they seem to find the synthetic stuff unpalatable. Manure, though, sets the temperature within the heap rising right away. Bill Bricker (the man who markets Kricket Krap) claims the reason is the bacteria and fungi already present in the natural product—they set decomposition in motion as soon as the manure is released into the moistened heap of organic matter.

Personally, I suspect that the difference in decomposition rates traces to the formulas of the two materials. The manure and the 5–10–5 contain the same nutrients, but in the synthetic fertilizer they have been formulated to suit the tastes of the plants. That is, the nutrients have been made to mimic the *end-products* of composting, the wastes that the decomposers leave behind. What the decomposing bacteria and fungi prefer to eat is the more complex compounds found in the manure (as well as the other undigested contents of the compost bin). What's a good diet for plants doesn't suit the decomposers, and vice versa.

Maybe. What I know for sure is that the compost that comes from my bin saves my Saturday mornings for me, and has drastically cut the expense of my horticultural habit. How?

I've got to get my bulbs into the ground, and my soil is almost entirely free of organic matter. All the topsoil was consumed by some tight-fisted Yankee farmer before he sold the exhausted field to a developer, I suppose. If there was any humus left at that point, then the developer probably followed the standard practice of scraping up the topsoil and selling it to a landscaper before he passed the property on to a homeowner.[1] Whatever the reason, there was no humus left in the yard by the time I bought it. So if I want my bulbs to perform as perennials, I have to dig in some organic material at planting time.

Without my compost heap, that would mean a trip

---

[1] I worked as a landscaper for a couple of years, and my mainstay was installing lawns at new developments. Inevitably I had to begin by covering the rock-hard moonscapes around each house with several inches of topsoil, and though I bought it from a middleman, I used to wonder if the homeowner was actually buying back from me the same material that had covered the same area originally. It became a lot less amusing when I myself bought a house and found my own topsoil being held for ransom.

to the garden center this morning. And when I did my pricing, what I found was this: ready-to-use organics are expensive, and the quality is poor.

Peat moss is the product that nurserymen have been pushing for the last half century. This is, according to my garden encyclopedia, "a carbonaceous substance formed by partial decomposition in water of various plants, especially sphagnum."[2] It's strip-mined from bogs and fens that took 10,000 years to form. My selfish concern at the garden center, however, was price, and I found that three cubic feet of this compressed brown fiber would cost me $10.79.

For that I would get enough of the stuff to treat approximately 150 square feet of garden bed. That's about half the area I could treat with one bin's-worth of compost. What the peat moss would accomplish, once I had mixed it into the soil, would be to bond with the clay, breaking that sticky mass up into crumbs — enough organic material will turn the heaviest clay into something like a chocolate cake — so that air and water can penetrate down to plant roots. Compost will accomplish the same things, and several more.

Peat moss, for instance, is sterile and has no nutrient value. Compost, by contrast, does release nutrients into the soil — though as noted in the preceding chapter, only in modest amounts. To be fair, there's some disagreement about the nutrient value of compost. Organic gardeners claim that their "black gold" has virtually everything a plant needs to grow, that it even contains some unspecified secret ingredients that actually make fruits and vegetables better tasting and more nutritious. Indeed, the true believers trace most of

---

[2]Donald Wyman, *Wyman's Garden Encyclopedia* (New York: Macmillan, 1986), p. 796.

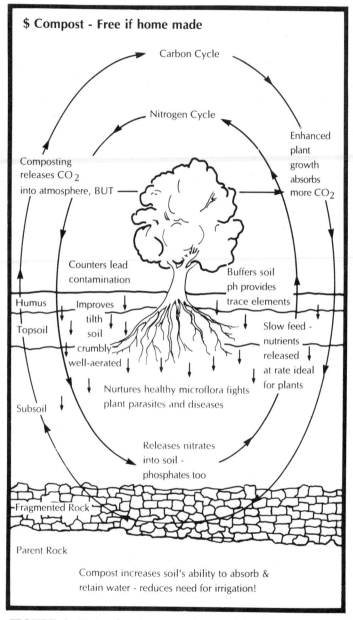

$ Compost - Free if home made

Carbon Cycle

Nitrogen Cycle

Composting releases CO_2 into atmosphere, BUT

Enhanced plant growth absorbs more CO_2

Counters lead contamination

Buffers soil ph provides trace elements

Humus

Topsoil

Improves tilth soil crumbly well-aerated

Slow feed - nutrients released at rate ideal for plants

Nurtures healthy microflora fights plant parasites and diseases

Subsoil

Releases nitrates into soil - phosphates too

Fragmented Rock

Parent Rock

Compost increases soil's ability to absorb & retain water - reduces need for irrigation!

FIGURE 6. Natural cycle versus the quick fix: how compost

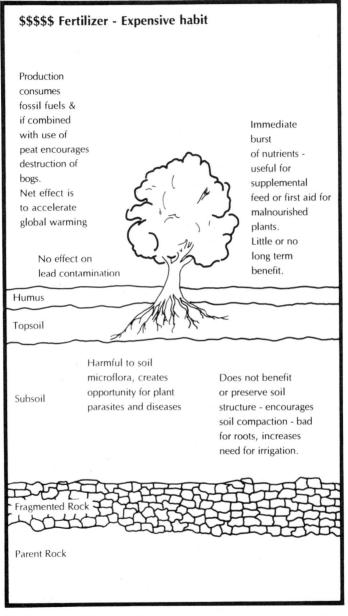

$$$$$ Fertilizer - Expensive habit

Production consumes fossil fuels & if combined with use of peat encourages destruction of bogs.
Net effect is to accelerate global warming

No effect on lead contamination

Immediate burst of nutrients - useful for supplemental feed or first aid for malnourished plants.
Little or no long term benefit.

Humus

Topsoil

Harmful to soil microflora, creates opportunity for plant parasites and diseases

Does not benefit or preserve soil structure - encourages soil compaction - bad for roots, increases need for irrigation.

Subsoil

Fragmented Rock

Parent Rock

compares to off-the-shelf fertilizers. (Guess our preference.)

humanity's ills to the consumption of chemically nourished foods.

As scientists, agriculturists rightly dismiss any claims composters may make for nutrients that they cannot identify. In the past, many refused to classify compost as a fertilizer at all. Instead, they call it a "soil conditioner." It's true that compost, pound for pound, contains only a fraction of the nutrients found in commercial fertilizers. But a crude comparison of this kind doesn't give a fair picture of compost's contribution to soil fertility.

The fertilizers you find down at the garden center are designed to give plants a quick, powerful jolt. Even the so-called slow-release organics spill out their nutrients in a matter of weeks, and many synthetics (some "organics," too) have a life of just days. Top-dress the garden with urea, and perhaps 10 to 30 percent of the nitrogen will escape as gaseous ammonia. Much of the rest may wash away, perhaps to help choke a river or lake with water weeds and algae, or perhaps penetrate down to the water table, where it will poison the water in your well.

Compost won't do either of those things. It releases its modest budget of nutrients a little at a time as it continues to decay in the soil. As a result, its effect lasts until the humus all decomposes, and as we noted in the last chapter, that may not happen for centuries. Compost doesn't overwhelm the plant, so very few of its benefits are wasted. This gives compost an impact disproportionate to the numbers.

Indeed, because humus bonds chemically with nitrates and ammonia (as well as phosphoric acid and potassium), compost will help keep nutrients in your soil. Compost not only releases nutrients at a more manageable rate, but also works actively to keep them within reach of the plant, thus protecting the environment from the poisonous effects of our fertilizers.

But to return to the contrast between compost and store-bought organic matter: peat moss does have an acidifying effect on the soil, and this was formerly a big selling point. Peat moss's own pH (the standard measure of a material's relative acidity) ranges down as far as 3.6 (strongly acidic) and so an admixture of peat moss tends to make a garden soil as a whole more acid. This was seen as an advantage a generation ago, since many plants—notably those suburban standbys, rhododendrons and azaleas—prefer a somewhat acidic soil, one with a pH of around 5.5.

With the spread of acid rain, however, this property of peat moss has ceased to be an advantage. Now that every storm bathes the garden in an acid solution, soils in most populated areas are acidic enough for any plant. In fact, the common problem east of the Mississippi and locally in broad areas of the Pacific Northwest, upper Midwest, and Southwest is that of keeping the soil from becoming *too* acidic. Compost, if made properly, generally tests neutral (pH 7.0 —neither acidic nor alkaline), and thus supplies the organic material a garden needs without worsening the imbalance created by acid rain.

Actually, the humus that compost supplies acts as a buffer, moderating the effect any input has on soil pH. If it weren't for the organic matter already in your soil, the application of such common materials as fertilizers and lime would cause wild swings in the pH, swings that would be fatal to many of your plants.

There are other organic materials available at garden centers besides peat moss, of course. During the four years I lived and gardened in central Texas (in my precomposting days), I used to buy composted pine bark for about $3 a bag. It took 18 bags of that to equal the volume of what I now produce in one batch of compost (my bins hold a cubic yard each). I didn't see composted bark at my garden center here in Connecticut, but I did see bags of fresh, shredded bark selling for $4.49. I could invest $80.82 in that, spread it over the garden, and wait a couple of years for it to decompose. Or I could put away my checkbook and wait six weeks for a bin of compost to mature.

Moving South—

Do you tire of tales of Connecticut? Why should someone like you—who lives in Phoenix—care about the horticultural problems of someone who wasn't smart enough to leave northern winters behind?

To begin with, your soil was deficient in organic matter even before the landscaper got hold of it. Because vegetation is sparse in the desert, there isn't much of anything to drop leaves and twigs—raw organic material—onto the soil surface. As soon as you begin watering any southern soil, too, the combination of warmth and moisture creates ideal circumstances for the breakdown of organic matter, so that what humus you have got begins to disappear. Your soil's appetite for organic matter is truly ravenous.

Hans Jenny, the giant of modern soil science, once analyzed soils from upstate New York to Georgia and Florida, and discovered that along this north–south line, an increase of 10° Celsius (that's equal to 18° Fahrenheit) in the average annual temperature was typically accompanied by a two-thirds decrease in the average organic content of a soil. Around Syracuse, New York, he found a loamy soil to contain, on average, 2.8 percent organic matter; by Mobile, Alabama, the level had dropped to 0.81.

I learned this truth the hard way in central Texas. The soil around our house in College Station was a sticky gray clay—and that color is a sure sign of the absence of humus. So the first spring I bought a truckload of spent compost from a nearby mushroom farm, spread it over the vegetable garden in a layer 4 inches deep, and spaded it in.[3] By fall, every sign of the mushroom compost was gone. I repeated the dose the following spring, and that disappeared just as rapidly. After four such treatments, any northern soil would have been granular, loose, and richly black. My Texas soil was extremely productive—I was harvesting all the vegetables my wife and I could eat out of 200 square feet of beds—but powdery and still gray.

I've since learned from soil scientists that southern soils simply do not accumulate organic matter and humus to the extent that northern ones do, especially in a garden. Yet they need it just as much. Indeed, in areas where water is in short supply, they need it even more. At least, the gardeners need the humus, for it is what stands between them and confiscatory water bills.

Water Conservation

Droughts have been much in the news in recent years, and the reporters' tendency has been to play up their catastrophic aspects. That makes good copy, and I could easily add my own horror stories. I visited Santa Barbara

---

[3] I highly recommend this lazy style of composting. The mushroom plant brewed its manure from an arcane mixture of chicken manure, wheat straw, peat moss, gypsum, lime, crushed feathers, cottonseed meal, and peanut meal. The result, by the time that it had produced its crop of mushrooms, smelled pleasantly like molasses and it worked a remarkable, if temporary, transformation on my leaden soil. All the hard work of composting—the mixing, turning, and so on—had been done by the plant employees and since I was doing the plant a favor—hauling away its waste—I was charged only $10 per pickup load. For that fee the plant shoveled it into my truckbed, too. Oh, that I still lived in mushroom country!

in 1991, for example, and spoke to a gardener there who was paying $500 per month just to keep the plants on her three-quarters of an acre alive. She is a landscape architect, and uses her own garden to advertise her work. She had to irrigate, no matter what it cost.

But to treat droughts as catastrophic is, more often than not, misleading. Meteorologists point out that in many areas (southern California, for example) such events are not unforeseen disasters, but instead regular features of the natural regime. It is we who have turned the droughts into catastrophes by trying to live as if they didn't occur. Santa Barbara is naturally a semidesert, not a tropical paradise, and trying to turn it into Tahiti was a sure prescription for trouble. And though we gardeners like to think of ourselves as stewards of the land, when it comes to water consumption we are the worst offenders. Typically, more than half of all water used by residential customers in the arid West is sprinkled onto the landscape.

Communities all over the West have begun encouraging landscaping more appropriate to the climate, either through education or, in the case of Los Angeles, through new building codes. The result has been an explosion of diversity in garden design. In each locale, a different type of planting is proving appropriate; that's not surprising, since the exact combination of climate and soil found in each region is unique, too. But in the midst of all the experimentation, the benefits of compost have always been crucial.

Compost aids water conservation in two ways. First, because it makes a soil lighter, crumbly and airy, compost makes it easier for soils to absorb water. Rain that falls on a compost-rich soil soaks in and down to where it is available to the plant roots. By contrast, rain may never penetrate the slick surface of a compacted and dense, organic-poor soil, so that it runs off downhill and is lost. So compost helps plants get the maximum benefit from natural precipitation, and that reduces the need for irrigation.

In addition, compost helps soils retain water. Like tiny sponges, the particles of compost each absorb up to twice their own weight in water, and then retain the moisture until it is in turn absorbed by roots. In short, compost acts as a kind of reservoir, storing water in times of abundance for use in times of scarcity. This is especially important in sandy or rocky soils where most of the water deposited by storms or sprinklers would otherwise drain rapidly down and through, beyond the reach of the plants. But in virtually any garden soil, an addition of compost will help to minimize waste and lengthen the interval between waterings. As my acquaintance in Santa Barbara can testify, that can translate into big savings.

Now I hear my neighbors in Connecticut dismissing this advice as useless to them—they may have winters, but they aren't short of water. And they aren't; not yet. But they'll have to irrigate more sparingly if the suburbs continue to explode. For as in most growing population centers across the country, the demand for water will eventually increase beyond the capacity of the existing supply system. When that happens, residents usually find that expanding the system is prohibitively expensive. The cities of Austin, Texas, and Denver, Colorado, and most of south Florida are learning to garden more conservatively for just that reason; so is Long Island, New York. In all those places, gardeners are finding compost extremely economical, a conservator of water and money that costs—nothing.

Healthy Soil Makes Healthy Plants— and Healthy Gardeners

It should be clear by now that I am not an organic gardener. Marty is, but I refuse to take the pledge. But even if I personally won't give up chemicals altogether, still I believe that the organic gardening movement can take credit for one of the most important horticultural advances of the last generation.

While agriculturists and horticulturists were treating the soil as nothing more than a matrix for nutrients and water, an inert anchor for plant roots, organic gardeners began focusing on its biology. The creatures you find in healthy soils, all the crawlers, burrowers, bacteria, and fungi, are more than bystanders, they insisted. It's due to their prodding, too, that scientists have come around to a more balanced view of the subject. Virtually everyone agrees now that the lives of all organisms growing in and on a particular plot are interconnected. Healthy plants are the product of healthy soils.

Organic gardeners were also correct in maintaining that organic matter—particularly humus—promotes this good health. You can, of course, grow plants without humus. You can grow them without even soil for that matter, as they do at the hydroponic farms, and harvest some pretty good Boston lettuce (I've eaten it, and as far as I can tell suffered no ill effects). The process is tricky, though, and it takes a lot of management. It's far easier to leave the supervision to compost.

Because compost works on many fronts simultaneously. Not only does it supply fuel to what ecologists call the microflora and microfauna (all the decomposers) and nurture your plants in all the ways discussed earlier, compost also helps to cleanse the soil, suppressing toxins, parasites, and diseases. The ways in which it does this are only beginning to be understood. But the effectiveness is increasingly clear.

What seems to be the key to compost's action against plant parasites and diseases is the bacteria and fungi it supports. There has been for a long time anecdotal evidence for the ability of composts to protect plants from fungal diseases such as root rots and damping off—diseases that are a terror to greenhouse operators and farmers and that may not sound familiar to you but that probably explain a lot of the mortality in your yard. This has caught the attention of a number of researchers, most notably Dr. Harry Hoitink of Ohio State University.

What he has observed is that plant pathogens—the microorganisms harmful to plants—do flourish in the compost heap, but only for the first two to four weeks after it is stacked, wetted, and set to work. After that, they are gradually edged out by saprophytes, organisms that feed specifically on dead and decaying organic material. The saprophytic bacteria and fungi displace pathogens by beating them in the struggle for nutrients—by starving the pathogens, saprophytes don't give them the chance to grow and reproduce. The pathogens that survive this struggle soon fall prey to micropredators, microorganisms that while harmless to higher plants do attack and kill pathogens. Finally, yet another class of beneficial microorganism gives the compost (and the soil in which you mix it) lasting protection from pathogens. This last group releases growth hormones into the compost, chemicals that favor higher plant growth and discourage that of the microundesirables.

Properly made composts are full of the good guys, and are being used all over the world as a treatment for soil-borne plant diseases, though to date largely on an experimental basis. Researchers at Taiwan's Chung Hsing University, for example, have used composts to control the fungus that causes watermelon wilt—and also bacteria that cause a variety of blights, yellows, and wilts of several other vegetables. In the San Joaquin Valley of California, a vintner found that spreading compost through the vineyard dramatically reduced the number of nematodes in his soil; the normal treatment for these plant-parasitizing worms is to cover the soil with a plastic sheet and fumigate with toxic gases, but the compost seems to have seeded the soil with fungi that strangle nematodes in their rootlike mycelia.

One commercial application of this discovery has been the compost-based potting mixes that greenhouse suppliers are making available to their customers. Growers of poinsettias, cyclamens, chrysanthemums, and many other plants are finding that the use of these "suppressive" potting mixes allows them to raise their crops without the fungicidal drenches they formerly were obliged to apply.

More pertinent to the needs of the average home-owner is the work of a plant pathologist at Cornell University, Eric Nelson. He has been using compost and the "antagonists" it breeds to protect turf against fungal diseases. In his tests, monthly applications of as little as 10 pounds of compost per 1,000 square feet of lawn (applied throughout the growing season) protected the turf against virtually every fungal disease for which he was watching.[4]

Both Hoitink and Nelson (and every other researcher in the field, for that matter) have found that not all composts are equal in their effectiveness. Nelson emphasizes that to encourage the production of beneficial fungi it is essential to maintain aerobic conditions within the heap, by turning it and by taking care not to soak it with water. A neglected heap of brush and weeds won't produce true compost, and so won't support the right microorganisms.

---

[4]The complete list is brown patch, dollar spot, gray snow mold, pythium blight, pythium root rot, red thread, southern blight, and take-all patch.

Even this kind of care, however, doesn't guarantee colonization by antagonists. Commercially produced composts, for instance, are commonly lacking in the beneficial microorganisms. That's because they are processed typically on sterile concrete pads or indoors in sealed cookers and kept free of infection, either good or bad. A number of research laboratories are working on "inoculants," cultures that could be applied to compost to seed them with the beneficial microorganisms. But Dr. Hoitink notes that the home composter can accomplish the same result with a handful of leafmold from the nearest woods—he has found that antagonists are common in woodland soils. Just wait until the heap has passed the hot stage and the compost is maturing, and sprinkle it with the well-rotted leaves and twigs. If your heap lies next to a wooded area, then according to Dr. Hoitink, you needn't bother even with that. If there are antagonists already in the soil, they will find their way up into the heap without help.

Jiminy!

They are more than just fish bait, Bill Bricker insists. Although the majority of Georgia's annual harvest of two billion crickets ends up on hooks, plenty go to feed reptiles, goldfish, and hummingbirds. Hummingbirds in captivity need crickets to eat in order to molt. Monkeys lo-o-o-ve crickets. And so does Bill Bricker.

He had retired as a colonel in 1977 after twenty-seven years in the infantry, and was looking for a business. The owner of a local garden center with whom he traded suggested that Bill ought to look first in his own backyard. His friend knew that Bill was mixing leaves, grass clippings, and horse manure to turn out a ton of compost each day. All this was going to rescue the plantings in his own yard with its 11-foot-deep layer of sand.

But as his friend pointed out, Bill could sell the stuff, too, for there were lots of neighbors in the same fix.

How had he developed his enthusiasm for composting? He'd grown up with it on the farm in Radbury, Virginia, that his father, a policeman, ran in his spare time. To the intimate knowledge of manures and other materials he gained there, Bill added a theoretical understanding through classes in agriculture at Virginia Tech. Later, he continued to garden, and compost, at every place the army stationed him: Germany, Thailand, Georgia, even Vietnam. In Southeast Asia, he struggled to grow tomatoes and lettuce, the homely stuff he couldn't find in local markets and missed. Compost wasn't enough there; he had to air-condition a greenhouse to bring in a crop of iceberg lettuce. But compost was plenty in Georgia, especially after he discovered cricket manure.

When he went into composting full time, Bill had taken on as a partner his former operations officer, Ed Hensley. Together they bought a site outside of Augusta where they began collecting wastes. The town was happy to get rid of chipped tree trimmings and grass clippings, a local stockyard kicked in a supply of paunch manure—material flushed from the cows' guts—and a stew factory sent truckloads of carrot and potato (or is *potatoe* more politically correct now?) peelings. The modest tipping fees Bricker and Hensley charged the suppliers (far less than that the landfill charges) made the operation almost profitable. Production really took off, though, after Bill discovered cricket manure.

When someone suggested he add this to the mix, Bill laughed. But he got serious fast as soon as he conducted the first trial. Applied to the garden straight, it raised test beds of tomato vines far sturdier and more productive than those fed on the synthetic fertilizer on which Bill had formerly relied. When added to the ever expanding windrows of compost, it "excited" them as nothing ever had before. Indeed, to keep the beds from overheating (temperatures above 160°F, Bill says, leave the compost "kinda scorched"), the partners began adding powdered granite. Even so, they finish a batch within fourteen days of the original mixing.

The campaign the two former infantrymen are waging has made their products — "compost-tost, breakfast for flowers"; "rosetost"; and the raw material, the cricket manure — a byword among gardeners, organic and otherwise. They produce 100 tons of compost each day now, using 6 to 10 tons of cricket manure a week. Last year they sold 3,000 cubic yards to a single customer, a tree nursery.

The straight manure, Bill notes, never moved under the original title, "CC-84." Not until his wife renamed it "Kricket Krap" did it really begin to sell. For three long years, the phone company refused to carry an unexpurgated advertisement in the Yellow Pages, and Rotary International still won't list it in *The Rotarian*. Bill doesn't care. "Those people who say Kricket Krap is anything more than cricket crap, well, they just have dirty minds."

He's found there's a living in composting, and it's one that he likes. "I'm lots happier composting than I was working as a hired gun. I'd much rather grow things and make things come to life." From his farm in Augusta, he shares not only products such as the quick composting system (twelve days, start to finish) with gardeners all over the country, but also advice.

"Soil in, air out," is one of his axioms — his experience has been that layering the materials in the heap with soil is not only unnecessary but harmful, because it tends to create anaerobic conditions. When that happens, "it putrefies, and when it putrefies, you start smellin' it, and that's all your richness leavin' there."

He also advises against piling the materials in layers,

as is classically recommended by organic gardeners. Because the carbon materials must join with the nitrogen-rich materials to compost, why not begin by mixing them thoroughly? To wet the pile (and failure to moisten the materials thoroughly is, he maintains, the number one reason for failure among home composters), he recommends soapy water, since soap reduces the water's surface tension and gives it greater penetrating power.

Any organic soap will work, though Bill stocks a yucca-based product from Mexico that he says is full of micronutrients. He uses an ounce to every gallon of water and applies it with a hose-end sprayer. This is something he's just begun doing, though actually it's an old trick.

"I learned that in years gone by, and just forgot about it, watching my grandmother put the soap and water, the dishwater, on her plants. She'd throw one bucket out, straight forward on her plants, and she'd throw one bucket to the left and one to the right. Then my grandpa would be fightin' her for the fourth one to take to his giant tomata. I'm lookin' at him right here [in a photograph on his office wall], and he's on a, oh, 8-foot step ladder, he was 6 foot 3 inches, and he's about 3 feet from the top of the tomata." Who can argue with results like those? But with two billion chirping neighbors, how does Bill Bricker sleep nights?

"Organic" Versus "Chemical" Fertilizers

This distinction is central to the creed of organic gardening, and because organic gardening looms so large in the composting world, it's worth examining.

To begin with, the distinction between the two kinds of fertilizers is an artifact—it is as man-made as any "chemical" fertilizer. The truth is that plants can absorb nutrients only in certain chemical forms, and if a fertilizer delivers them in another form, then the plants must wait for decay or weathering to reduce the "foods" to one they can use. Can a plant distinguish between the nitrate (NO_3-) that it gets from a bacterium's or fungus's digestion of manure and a chemically identical compound that happens to come from a factory? I don't see how, but a strict organic gardener will use one and not the other.

Exactly what an "organic" fertilizer is I have never been able to determine. A chemist's definition of organic is that the compound contains organic carbon — they exclude from this company only "elemental" carbons such as diamond, graphite, or carbon dioxide gas. Organics of this kind can be manufactured as easily by a chemist as by a cow, and they include not only plastic soda bottles and polyester leisure suits but also many of the most notorious pesticides, such as DDT.

The definition that organic gardeners seem to favor is an obsolete, nineteenth-century one that classifies as organic any compound derived from a plant or animal source. But with this group they include many things that never were alive. Granite meal and greensand are favorite sources of potassium for organic gardeners, even though both are minerals.

Rock phosphate, one of their favorite phosphorus fertilizers, would not be classified as organic by a chemist, but at least it owes its birth in some unspecified fashion to ancient marine organisms. The phosphate found in this rock is, as it comes from the mine, water insoluble, so that it is useless to a plant until it has been broken down by acids in the soil. Yet should a chemist anticipate nature by treating rock phosphate with sulfuric acid, the result, so-called superphosphate, has somehow become inorganic, or at least unacceptable to organic gardeners.

Ultimately, the guiding principle seems to be suspicion of technology and anything not of natural origin. That's a suspicion I share, for the chemical industry has a checkered history and continues to mislead the public whenever it is profitable to do so. Yet why should by-products of the meat-packing industry be any healthier than those of a chemical plant? Feed lots and the floods of manure they generate are one of America's worst sources of water pollution; what environmental price do we pay for the blood-and-bone meal organic gardeners endorse so enthusiastically? I suspect the environmental cost of a bag of synthetic nitrates is far less.

Do I want to eat food full of toxic chemicals? No — though I recognize that plants are themselves great manufacturers of pesticides, and that some of those products (the cyanides in various fruit tree pits and seeds, for example, or the deadly alkaloid solanine, contained by many members of the tomato-potato family) are highly toxic too. I avoid spraying my vegetable garden with any pesticide stronger or more persistent than soap.

I also agree with the organic gardeners that because chemical fertilizers don't replace organic matter, relying entirely on such products will impoverish the soil. But I don't hesitate to sprinkle a modest measure of 5–10–5 onto my well-composted beds at planting time. Does this injure the microorganisms in my soil, as organic gardening colleagues claim? I can't say for sure, but the tangles of earthworms I find there obviously do not mind.

Saving $ While Saving the Peat Bogs

What is peat? It's partially decayed vegetable matter — leaves, stems, and roots of all sorts of plants that have accumulated in water-logged conditions, where decomposers cannot get the oxygen they need to proceed.

Practically speaking, though, it's the horticultural equivalent of aspirin—it's the medicine for every disease.

Your garden center recommends it as the cure for too-heavy clay soils, and too-loose sandy ones. You should mix it with the soil around the trees and shrubs you plant, to protect them from drought. You should add it to your potting soils to keep them from compacting, and you should sprinkle it over the lawn as a top-dressing to promote better tilth. All the promotion has worked: peat is the only organic matter most of us ever administer to our yard or garden.

It's little wonder we use so much of it. Besides the 750,000 or so tons we import from Canada every year, Americans mine about a million tons from their own bogs. Although actually, industry spokespeople prefer to use the word "harvest" now for what they do. This suggests peat is a resource that is renewing itself.

That seems to be true in Canada. That country possesses vast tracts of bogs: 278 million acres, and it takes peat from just 40,000 of these (0.02 percent of the total). But if Canada is rich in this resource, it is also taking care to use what it has wisely. In 1988 producers there organized the Canadian Sphagnum Peat Moss Association, a trade group that promotes the harvesting of bogs in a sustainable manner. Removal of peat in a particular bog is stopped while a thick layer of the original material still remains; strips of vegetation are left undisturbed through harvested areas so that plants and animals can recolonize; and water levels (which are lowered during harvesting) are restored. The result is that bogs do seem to regenerate, and the Canadian producers figure that they are removing peat at less than one-sixtieth the rate at which it is accumulating.

The situation is very different in the United States. We have a smaller area of peatlands—perhaps 100 million acres, about half of which lie in Alaska and are commercially inaccessible. Peat harvesting is regulated only minimally—appropriately, it falls under the jurisdiction of the Bureau of Mines, since the federal government regards peat as a fossil fuel. Deposits are commonly strip-mined until exhausted. Florida is the number one state in peat production, and there the former peatlands are not restored but instead "reclaimed" for use as crop- or pastureland. This of course exposes to the air whatever peat remains, with the result that it oxidizes. It slow-burns right in place, and while the burn is slow by comparison to a real fire, it's fast enough that within forty years, large areas of what were once Everglades will be bare rock.

The worst part of this is that the peat we harvest domestically isn't nearly the quality of the imported product. Canadian peat is sphagnum peat, the semidecayed remains of sphagnum mosses. It holds up to thirty times its own weight in water and is 95–99 percent organic matter. It's sterile, even mildly antiseptic, and when added to potting soils has been proven to deter several of the bacteria and fungi that attack and kill germinating seeds and seedlings.

Most of the U.S. product is lower-quality sedge peat—peat from miscellaneous plants—or the heavily decayed humus peat. These lack most of the sphagnum peat's virtues. Sedge peat, for instance, holds water only half as well as the sphagnum peat, while humus peat may be as little as 20 percent organic matter and has no special water-holding capacity. The peat industry itself tacitly acknowledges the difference in quality. Whereas the Canadian peat commonly sells pure, in bales by itself, the inferior U.S. peat generally finds industrial uses—as an additive in packaged potting soils or pressed into peat pots and pellets. There's nothing very special about the U.S. peat; certainly, nothing special enough to warrant the destruction of our peat-lands.

Botanists can provide long lists of fascinating and rare species—pitcher plants and Venus flytraps, orchids and bladderworts—that flourish only in peat bogs and fens, and hunters know how important they are to waterfowl. Bogs and fens also supply a crucial piece of the system that regulates the water supply; the peatlands act as sponges, flood regulators, and filters. In addition, they absorb and store huge amounts of carbon, effectively reducing the amount of CO_2 in the atmosphere by half. This has caused Lee F. Clinger, a geographer at the National Center for Atmospheric Research in Boulder, Colorado, to propose a link between the history of peatlands—their expansion and contraction—to the warming and cooling of the earth's climate. Is your need to improve your garden soil worth aggravating the greenhouse effect?

Think of the trailer truckloads of peat coming *in* from the bogs—and the truckloads of organic matter headed *out* to the landfill. Do the drivers wave as they pass on the highway? Wouldn't it make more sense to leave each material, as much as possible, in place?

We're not suggesting that you give up peat altogether. Real sphagnum peat is the best material in which to sow seeds or root cuttings. But don't substitute it for compost when you are simply replacing organic matter. And when you do buy peat, look for a maple leaf symbol, and the words "Canadian Sphagnum Peat Moss."

Compost as Middleman

If soil scientists are unwilling to accept the existence of secret ingredients, that doesn't mean they deny compost's special nutritive value. Compost, they agree, may be low in nutrients itself, but the humus it supplies can make available to plants nutrients already in the soil through its "chelating" effect.

Chēlē, or as it is properly written "chlh," is the ancient Greek word for a crab's claws, and that's how humus behaves in the presence of certain metals, reaching out to grab and envelop them. Metals such as iron, zinc, copper, and manganese are essential to plant growth — chlorophyll, for instance, the stuff that makes plants green and allows them to manufacture food from sunlight, contains magnesium. Yet in their native forms the metals may be indigestible. Like the sugar coating on a pill, the chelating humus makes the minerals palatable, and so, though it doesn't actually furnish the nutrient, it does play an important supporting role in this essential type of nutrition.

That doesn't mean that if your plants suffer from mineral deficiencies (they too can develop iron-poor blood) you must supply compost. You can spray or sprinkle special "plant tonics," concentrates or the chelated minerals, and in very exceptional cases where the soil is actually deficient in the mineral, this may be the only solution. But tonics wash out of the soil, and at $11.99 a bottle (at my garden center) they are an expensive habit. At least give compost a chance.

Protecting People, Too

Public health officials call it "the silent epidemic." They say that lead poisoning afflicts far, far more children than other, better known childhood diseases, and that it's not just a problem of urban areas. Old lead pipe plumbing is one source of this toxin, and paint chips or dust is another. But one of the most dangerous reservoirs of lead is the soil around our houses. The good news is that you can correct that with compost.

There are a number of ways in which your soil may have become tainted with lead. Lead was a common ingredient of house paints well into the 1970s, so that the flakes you scrape off while repainting may be poisoning your soil. Auto exhaust was also a major source of lead until the introduction of unleaded gasolines, so if your yard lies close to a busy road, chances are your soil got a dose that way. Even if you live *way* out in the country, you still may not be safe: lead arsenate was commonly applied to fruit trees as an insecticide from the 1890s into the 1950s, so old orchards are often heavily contaminated.

Parents with children under the age of 6 should take this threat especially seriously, since preschoolers are especially vulnerable. A daily dose of as little as a tenth of a gram of lead can cause brain damage in toddlers, who may not betray any symptoms of lead poisoning at the time. In part, children are especially at risk from lead-contaminated soils because they are more liable to put it in their mouths or get it on their hands and then swallow it with their food. But young children also absorb more of the lead they do ingest—as much as 70 percent, versus an adult's typical absorption rate of 10 to 40 percent.

Finding out if your soil is lead contaminated is relatively easy and inexpensive. The Yellow Pages (or your local cooperative extension agent) can direct you to environmental testing laboratories that will assay the soil sample you send them. Call around—when Tom wanted his soil tested, he found that prices ranged from as high as $200 to as little as $40.

If the test shows as much as 500 ppm (parts per million) of lead (and urban soils commonly test as high as 1,000 to 5,000 ppm), then you've got a soil that the EPA considers "hazardous." Lesser concentrations, such as the 225 ppm the lab found in Tom's soil, may still be of concern if you intend to grow your own vegetables—leafy greens such as lettuce and root crops such as carrots may absorb the lead and pass it on to the gardener at dinner.

Time was that the only treatment for lead-contaminated soils was to scrape off the top 6–8 inches and replace it with clean soil—a catastrophically expensive solution. That may still be indicated if your yard is severely contaminated—5,000 ppm or more. In less severe cases, though, like that 500 ppm, public health officials are now recommending compost.

A lot of compost: the recommendation is to bring your soil up to a level of 25 percent organic matter. This alleviates the lead contamination in two ways. First, it dilutes the problem soil, reducing the concentration of lead, so that the teaspoonful your child eats will contain 20 percent less of the toxin. More importantly, though, the humus bonds with the lead, making it less easily absorbed, so that much of the lead your child does ingest will pass through the digestive system harmlessly.

There's another benefit: compost will make your vegetables more wholesome, too. A USDA test found that mixing compost with contaminated soil reduced lead uptake by lettuce some 64 percent, and that of spinach, carrots, and beets by about 50 percent.[5] The bigger the dose of compost, the more pronounced was this effect. Researchers at Cornell University found that in soils with organic contents of 40–50 percent, there was no observable uptake of lead even when the lead contamination ran as high as 3,000 ppm.[6]

[5]"Sludge Beats Lead," *Organic Gardening,* February 1992, p. 19.
[6]Nina L. Bassuk, *Lead in Urban-Grown Vegetables,* New York State College of Agriculture and Life Sciences, Cornell University Urban Horticulture Institute, Ithaca, New York, July 19, 1983.

Does this mean that a dedicated composter can ignore the dangers of lead-contaminated soil? No. You should still have your soil tested, especially if you live in an older home, close to a busy road, or in an urban area. If the test indicates elevated lead levels, you should definitely consult public health officials or your state department of environmental protection. In the meantime, for safety's sake, be sure to keep composting.

CHAPTER 5

What's Compostable and What Isn't?

T HE SHORT ANSWER to that question is that anything organic (and we're using that term in the scientific sense) will compost, under the right conditions. There are a few things you'll find difficult to decompose, and others, well, you'll wish you hadn't. But these *are* few in number and easy to avoid, if you use a little common sense.

We (Marty and Tom) made a vow when we planned this book that we'd keep chemistry out of it. Our chemist friend David made us promise this, muttering something about a *very* little knowledge being a particularly dangerous thing. But it isn't possible to avoid chemistry altogether when discussing a chemical process. We've been on the telephone to him again, and are going to try and pass along in ungarbled form what he told us.

As we have already mentioned, it is the presence of

organic carbon (and we are using *organic* in that scientific sense again) that defines an organic material. Not surprisingly, decomposers need more of this carbon than any other nutrient—they use it as a cellular building block, besides consuming it as fuel. They need nitrogen, too, in lesser amounts, since that is an essential constituent of proteins, which are as important to a microorganism as they are to you. If the composting is to proceed quickly and smoothly, carbon and nitrogen must blend in a proportion that suits the decomposers' needs, and achieving that may involve some mixing of different materials. We'll get to that in the next chapter, but it's enough to note here that the recipes aren't at all exacting.

Besides carbon and nitrogen, decomposers need water. Every living thing does, after all. The desirable kind of decomposers, the aerobic ones, also need oxygen. But it's the composter who furnishes these two materials by sprinkling the heap and by stirring air into it.

Finally, in addition to these bulk items—water, oxygen, carbon, and nitrogen—the decomposers need a host of "micronutrients" too. These include a museum-full of minerals: cobalt, manganese, copper, molybdenum, and others, as well as sulfur, phosphorus, calcium, and potassium. They are all things that Marty and Tom have no idea how to obtain. Fortunately, the decomposers need only traces of them and they are supplied in adequate amounts by virtually any vegetable matter you may add to the heap.

So if you dump nitrogen and carbon—which are contained in the remains or waste of any living thing—into the compost bin, wet them and toss them like a salad, the decomposers will go to work? Probably. There are actually some organic compounds that are bound together so tightly and seamlessly that the decomposers may have great difficulty in prying them apart. Our chemist friend was explaining all about double bonds and single bonds and chemical "hooks" when we set the receiver down on the desk.

When we picked it up again, he had returned to ordinary, scientifically illiterate English, and was sharing examples of these hard-to-compost materials. We recognized benzene and paraffin. These, according to him, are both organic, and do derive (at least in their original, natural form) from living things. Under certain conditions, they, too, will compost. Indeed, the new field of bioremediation, the business of using microorganisms to clean up toxic wastes, is largely a special form of composting. It is being used to cleanse soil and water of all sorts of nasty organics, including a number of industrial solvents and insecticides. But no home composters have the skill or equipment to make this work, and anyway no composters in their right minds would add such materials to a backyard heap.

So if we rule out petrochemicals and insecticides, what does this leave that *is* compostable? All sorts of things, and some of them things that you might not think of right away. Marty and Tom compost the usual, of course. There's the peelings and parings from cooking, vegetable leftovers, grass clippings (if we let the lawn go too long between mowing). And so forth.

But they have also experimented with hair trimmings from the barbershop (that spooked the barber, and we don't think he believed our explanation about hair being about 15 percent pure nitrogen), cardboard, wood ashes, old newspapers, and every kind of manure from cricket to horse. But these things are the condiments. The meat and potatoes of our bins' diet are the organic wastes that are locally abundant and cheap.

In autumn, we fill their bins with fallen leaves. Dead leaves are one of New England's most abundant natural resources, and it's nice to derive something from them

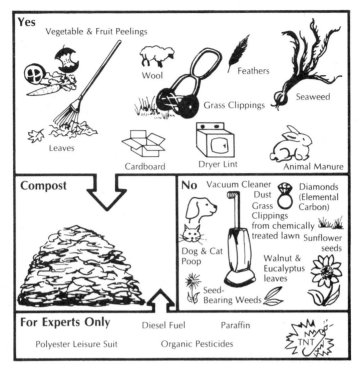

FIGURE 7. To compost or not to compost: a quick guide to your heap's diet.

besides blisters (from rake handles) and traffic jams (from the leaf-peeping tourists). In Texas, Tom used mushroom manure, which was already composted, but he could have used the cow chips from the agricultural school down the road (he decided not to when his environmentalist wife insisted they pack the harvest home by bicycle). We know people in Maine who live near woolen mills, and they compost waste wool; and a friend next to a pharmaceuticals plant swears by the mouse manure she gets from the animal lab (thorough composting should decompose the additives, but we wouldn't touch the stuff).

Marty lives a short drive from the beach and could easily fill his bins with seaweed, if he wasn't too busy bowling on Saturday mornings. Seaweed is actually richer in nitrogen than most manures and contains every imaginable trace element, and if you throw it on the heap you won't have to consume it as sushi. A ubiquitous resource, one we've never exploited but easily could, is the spoiled vegetables thrown out at the local supermarket. You could easily produce compost for a whole neighborhood from these, which is exactly what Star Markets is doing in Massachusetts.

A federally funded research project—the Sea Grant Program—has been composting fish wastes along the shores of Lake Huron. The managers of that program have been taking the scraps and heads that sport fishermen leave at fish-cleaning stations and mixing them with chipped brush—one part fish to four parts wood chips—and then burying the mess under 4 to 8 more inches of chips. These dedicated composters claim to have been producing a superior compost in just 6 to 8 weeks, and with no odor problems along the way. We still advise caution—the fish and chips attracted a black bear who adopted the warm heap as his bed.

Materials that come to us highly recommended by Marty's friends the organic gardeners (but which we've never tried personally) include the following:

Chicken feathers. Although adding these to the heap will increase the need for water, they are an exceptionally rich source of nitrogen, yielding an amount equal to about 15 percent of their total weight.

Beet wastes. Common in sugar beet country, especially rich in potassium (up to 4 percent by weight) and phosphorus (to 0.6 percent).

Felt waste. Available at hat factories, up to 14 percent nitrogen.

Leather dust. Up to 12 percent nitrogen, substantial amounts of phosphorus. A good material if there is a leather goods factory nearby.

Dryer lint. Why not? The chemical composition is obviously going to vary with your wardrobe, but if you prefer the natural feel of cotton, your lint is going to be rich in potassium.

Vacuum cleaner dust. This could be a problem if you own an older house since paint flakes or chips could add significant amounts of lead. Better let the garbage truck haul this away.

Straw and spoiled hay. Farmers give these materials away for a nominal price once molds or mildew get into the bales. Whereas fresh grass clippings are rich in nitrogen, this nutrient breaks down as the material dries so that straw and hay are mainly sources of carbon. To compost, you must mix them with a source of nitrogen such as clippings straight from the mower or an animal manure. Because straw and hay are light they help to keep the heap fluffy and well aerated.

Tobacco stems. This waste may be available locally in tobacco-growing areas, and composting is a healthy use (the *only* healthy use) for it. About 3 percent nitrogen, and as much as 7 percent potassium. Do not add tobacco in any form, however, to compost you intend to apply to the vegetable garden, since its wastes may host tobacco mosaic virus, a disease that *will* survive composting and that is devastating to tobacco relatives such as eggplants, tomatoes, and potatoes.

Sawdust. We keep meaning to try this since we could pick it up in bulk at a small lumber mill a few miles away. Like straw, sawdust is valuable primarily as a carbon source, and contains only about 0.1 percent nitrogen.

Mud. This may be a pollutant in a Midwestern stream and a problem when it accumulates in the reservoir, but it can be great stuff in your garden. Chinese farmers have relied for centuries on the muck they dredge from the beds of canals, composting it with layers of animal manures or freshly cut clover. Depending on what falls into the water, muck may contain significant amounts of nitrogen, phosphorus, and potassium, though it is likely to be deficient in carbon. One word of caution: make sure that your muck mine doesn't lie directly downstream from a factory, or in the watershed of a neighbor's chemically nourished lawn, since either one may fill the sediment with undesirable toxins.

Actually, the issue of toxic contaminants is one every composter should investigate before starting to experiment with any material. Ask the stable owners before you take home their horse manure to dump in your bin; they may have sprayed the horses' bedding with an insecticide to protect the horses from flies. If you want to compost the neighbors' grass clippings, ask if they have treated their lawns with insecticides or fungicides recently. A thorough, hot composting will degrade many such pesticides, but it won't affect many industrial solvents or toxic heavy metals such as lead or zinc, which are present in many industrial wastes. The best rule is, if in doubt, keep it out of the heap. Your aim is to restore your soil, not turn your yard into a Superfund site.

Overall, though, our advice is to be bold and experiment. Most composting mistakes sort themselves out with time. Tom should have chopped all those windfall apples he added to his bin last fall, and his failure to do so meant that they persisted—shriveling like shrunken heads but still recognizably fruits—long after the horse apples and shredded leaves around them disintegrated. But all Tom had to do was wait an extra few months before emptying the bin. When he tried composting cardboard, he didn't shred the carton into fine-enough pieces. As a result, the soggy brown pancakes took almost six months to degrade. In the end, though, they did.

To protect yourself from aggravation, though, you may want to exclude the following materials from the heap:

• *Tough, leathery leaves* such as those that fall from live oaks, hollies, or southern magnolias. These are often extremely resistant to decay. Tom discovered this in Texas when he tried sheet composting leaves from his live oak tree.

Sheet composting is a lazy method, one in which wastes are spread across the surface of the soil and then turned under to decompose in place. As the wastes decompose, they may absorb much of the soil's nitrogen, which will starve any plants growing on site. This effect is only temporary, however, as the wastes release the stolen nitrogen, with interest, as they finish decomposition. The usual way of handling this difficulty is to sheet compost in the fall, after harvest, since you can ordinarily count on the composting to be completed by spring.

Tom's live oak leaves had not decomposed significantly by the time he turned the soil for the spring crop. Indeed, they hadn't really begun to degrade by the time he and his wife sold the house three years later. Tom suspects that they may persist like those 2,000-year-old stiffs they dig out of peat bogs, though he is also confident that no one who finds the leaves later will care. The plants certainly didn't. The leaves' failure to decompose had an incidental benefit: they posed no temporary threat to the soil's fertility. Of course, they didn't benefit the plants, either.

• *Ripe weeds,* weeds that have gone to seed, may also cause you grief. If you compost hot and thoroughly, most of the seeds will be consumed. But a small percentage may survive—and a small percentage can be a lot, since some weeds produce 100,000 seeds per plant. Any survivors, of course, you will be sowing back into the yard wherever you spread the finished compost. So try to be conscientious in pulling the weeds and get them, if possible, before they set seed.

Of course, a failure to destroy all the seeds in your compost heap can bring its own reward. Despite all his fussing and turning, Tom failed to kill all the seeds from a cantaloupe he tossed into the bin. The heat from the decay helped the survivors germinate extra early and kept them alive through a late spring frost, so that Tom eventually picked several perfect melons from those vines.

• *Perennial weeds with tough, creeping stems and roots.* Anyone who has attempted to pull weeds such as these—quack grass, for example—from a garden bed knows how tough they are. Their roots are usually as durable as they are tenacious, and they can survive a prolonged burial in the cool, outer margin of a compost pile. This is especially true if you should add the roots to the heap in late autumn; then they may well survive in a dormant state right until spring.

If you keep the heap's interior at 150°F, and if you are thorough about turning and mixing the pile regularly, you will kill even the toughest roots. If your style of composting is more casual, though, be sure to toss into the trash, not the compost bin, any wiry roots you weed out of the lawn or garden. Otherwise, you will be once again spreading weeds with the compost, since whole new plants can sprout from bits of the weeds' roots.

Common weeds of this type include quack grass, Canada thistle, ox-eye daisies, ground ivy, Johnson grass, mugwort, and common Bermudagrass. Other persistent roots that can pose problems are the bulbs of field garlic (what we called *onion grass* when we were children) and the tubers of nutsedge.

• *Chemical warriors*—and we mean plants not people. Competition is even rougher in the plant world than in the human one—they are even more crowded than we are, and they have no choice but to stay and fight. There's one sure way for a vegetable to claim some elbow room, though, and that's to poison its neighbors. This is a very common practice, actually, and the more adept inflict it with a facility that would shame a Borgia.

These plant poisoners are known botanically as *allelopaths.* Either through secretions from their roots or by chemicals in the litter of old leaves and stems they drop around them, they suppress the germination of any seeds that fall nearby or even kill actively growing competitors. The group includes a surprising number of familiar species, including cucumbers and marigolds, but because composting usually destroys the allelopath's residues, most are of no concern to us. You won't harm your garden by tossing a bouquet of marigolds into the bin.

There are a few allelopaths, however, whose harmful effects do seem to survive composting. Anyone who has a black walnut in his or her yard knows how lethal this tree is; typically, it stands at the center of a broad circle of sparse and stunted vegetation. Its particular poison, juglone, will apparently persist in compost made from the tree's leaves, nuts, or sawdust.

You may have noticed, too, the circle of yellowed grass below the bird feeder—this results from the natural herbicide leaching out of the sunflower hulls those darned squirrels have dumped there. Obviously, it would be a mistake to rake this mess up and dump it into the bin, especially since the woody hulls are slow to break down. If everything else in the bin had degraded to brown crumbs, you might easily judge the compost finished and administer it to the plants with the sunflower hulls still unprocessed.

Without a doubt the most serious allelopathic threat occurs in California. One of the most common groups of trees through the southern and central parts of the state are eucalyptuses, and their litter might seem an ideal resource for the composter. It isn't. Because the foliage is full of oils, it resists decomposition, and it is harmful to the growth of a broad array of plants. If the town collects yard waste for composting, you might dispose of eucalyptus leaves that way, reasoning that they will be diluted in the great windrows of the municipal plant. Or you could use the leaves as mulch below the tree that shed them. Whatever you do, though, don't let them choke and pollute your compost heap.

A last reassurance — composting is by nature a cleansing process. Use a little common sense in what you add to your heap, and leave the really exotic organics to bioremediators. Follow the instructions in the next chapter for building your heap (they are simple and easy), and relax. The decomposers won't let you down.

Merde!

It was the original compostable, the raw material of those biblical dungheaps. There are reasons, too, why protorecyclers favored manure, besides the fact that it was everywhere they looked (and if they didn't look, they were sorry). Manure is predigested organic matter, organics that come already filled with decomposers and well along the way to compost.

Yet despite these obvious advantages, manure gets

short shrift in many modern gardening books. The authors may make a bow to its historic importance, but then dismiss the subject with a claim that most of their readers no longer have access to manure. They should check their facts.

The truth is that we are in the midst of a manure boom. While horses may have disappeared from our streets, and the average family no longer keeps its own cow, livestock still outnumbers humans five to one in the United States. As of 1989, for instance, there were 1.3 billion chickens scratching at the U.S. of A. and annually depositing 37 million tons of dung. Although there were only one-tenth as many cows, they dumped a load forty times greater, and we've still got 2.5 million horses, and almost as many goats. All in all, farms pile up more than 1.4 billion tons of manure every year.

In many cases, the farmers are only too glad to give this harvest away, too. With suburbia closing in around their farms, they can't dispose of this by-product by spreading it over their fields as their fathers did, and if they pile it up it's liable to leak nutrients into streams and bring in the pollution control officers. Factor in those people who keep herbivorous pets, whether ducks, bunnies, or those trendy pot-bellied pigs, and what you've got is a buyer's market.

Marty doesn't care for manure, but Tom considers himself a connoisseur, and though he lives in one of the most densely populated regions of the country, he's never yet run short. He gets his manure gratis, and he doesn't drive more than a couple of miles to pick it up. This means he must be flexible—he's got to take what he can get—but he's never encountered a manure he didn't like.

There are, however, very definite differences among the different types. Cow manure is the most fully digested—before the organics land in this pie, they pass

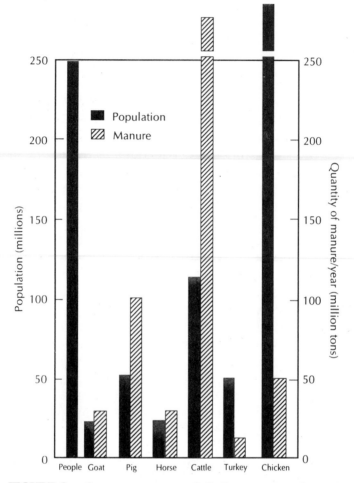

FIGURE 8a. So you say you can't find any manure for your heap? Our excremental census suggests you just aren't looking very hard.

	%Nitrogen	%Phosphate	%Potash
Cow	0.50	0.20	0.50
Horse	0.60	0.20	0.50
Sheep	1.00	0.30	1.00
Chicken	1.50	0.75	0.50
Rabbit	2.40	1.40	0.60

FIGURE 8b. And while we're on the subject: what is the most nutritious manure, from a plant or decomposer's point of view? Listed above are the percentages by weight of macronutrients (nitrogen, phosphorus, and potassium) found in commonly available manures.

through four stomachs—which makes it relatively low in nutrients, but easy for decomposers to digest. Horse manure is somewhat richer in nitrogen—whereas cow contains an average of 0.5 percent nitrogen, 0.2 percent phosphorus, and 0.5 percent potassium, horse tests at 0.6–0.2–0.5. Sheep is even "hotter" (as the old-timers put it): 1.0–0.3–1.0; while chicken manure comes in tops at 1.5–0.75–0.5. Still, it's rabbit manure that's the real premium product: 2.4–1.4–0.6.

All these values apply only to fresh manures—many of the nutrients wash away if the material is left out in the rain. Anyway, nutrient content is only one measure of a manure's value. Also important is its organic content, which may be as low as 14 percent (in pig manure) or 33 percent in rabbit or sheep.[1] Another benefit of manure is the things that come with it, specifically, the decomposers. Herbivore manure comes already well seeded with spores and eggs of the mites, bugs, bacteria,

---

[1]These figures come from two sources: William Bryant Logan's article, "Get Some Manure into Your Life," *Organic Gardening,* April 1992; and *The Rodale Book of Composting* (Emmaus, PA: Rodale Press, 1992).

and fungi that will decompose it in the heap or bin—this living freight may compose 30 percent of the total mass.

This makes manure composting unusually quick and easy, particularly in the case of cow manure, whose proportion of carbon to nitrogen is close to ideal. Cow manure you don't have to mix with anything else—dump into a bin, turn it a couple of weeks later to aerate it, and remove good compost a couple of months later.

One caveat: You should *not* add cat manure to your compost heap, nor that of dogs or even pet birds. All these may contain germs or parasites dangerous to you and your neighbors, and these pathogens will survive anything but the kind of hot and thorough processing they receive in a commercial composting plant.

For the same reason, human manure is unsuitable for the home heap, though urine, curiously, is not. As long as you are healthy, the water you make should be germ free, and we know at least one rather buttoned-down publishing executive who on fine nights strolls out to the compost bin to pee. He's got rural roots, so outdoor plumbing doesn't fluster him and he loves his wife, a superb gardener who depends absolutely on her homemade compost. Besides, to stand legs astraddle under the silence and the stars lets him be, for a minute anyway, as carefree and full of wonder as a boy on a camping trip once again.

Good Enough to Eat?

There's gold in seaweed—only 0.000006 percent, not enough to interest a miner, but there's gold there all the same, and silver and platinum too. More importantly, though, from a composter's perspective, there's cobalt, manganese, copper, molybdenum, calcium, and all the other micronutrients healthy compost (and healthy soils) need. In short, seaweed is far too valuable to waste on human consumption.

In fact, in a comparison with manure, seaweed emerges as clearly superior, at least as a food for decomposers. The classic source for the seaweed-composting industry, *Seaweed in Agriculture & Horticulture,* lists seaweed's organic content at 400 pounds per ton—20 pounds more than you'd get from the typical ton of farmyard manure. Seaweed typically exceeds manure in nitrogen content, and although it is somewhat poorer in phosphorus, seaweed contains almost double the amount of potassium, a nutrient that promotes strong leaf and stem growth, as well as improving flower, fruit, and seed production, so seaweed should be of benefit in both flower and vegetable gardens, as well as on the lawn.

Seaweed is that rarest of combinations—a commodity of great value that remains abundant and cheap. Almost every storm leaves it in a thick windrow at the high-tide mark, and no one is going to complain if you haul it away. Poor farmers (and thrifty ones, too) have traditionally relied on it to renew their soil; indeed, on the Aran Islands, off the west coast of Ireland, seaweed often *is* the soil. On the barren terraces of those islands, farmers lay down alternate layers of seaweed and sand onto the rock to create the beds in which they grow their potatoes, and after a spud harvest or two, all their other vegetables, as well.

The one potential problem with seaweed (and the reason that the Aran Islanders wait a few seasons before planting anything other than the hardy potato into new beds) is the fresh seaweed's coating of salt. You can easily cure that, though, by leaving your gatherings stacked on the driveway until a rainstorm has washed off the sea water.

Because seaweed is relatively rich in nitrogen, it's

particularly valuable to any compost maker who relies on such carbon-rich materials as sawdust, hay, or autumn leaves. Actually, you should always try to mix seaweed with some carbon source as you add it to the bin. Otherwise, your heap may begin exhaling nitrogen in the form of ammonia (see the next chapter for a fuller discussion of this problem), which robs the finished compost of some nutrient value, and may make your heap unpleasant to handle in the meantime. Combining one part leaves or hay or sawdust with every two parts seaweed will ensure that this unfortunate situation never occurs.

Why doesn't Marty take advantage of the seaweed bonanza that lies just blocks from his doorstep? Tom suspects the reason is that Marty actually likes sushi. It's a pity, in Tom's opinion, that a seaside address should be wasted on an individual of such poor judgment.

Paperwork

It's organic, it degrades readily, and it makes up 40 percent by volume of what goes to the landfill—paper would seem to be the ideal compostable. Of course we support paper composting—didn't you read the title? But before you rush the junk mail out to the heap, be aware of the problems.

First of all, you are going to enrage the neighborhood environmentalists if you compost papers that are recyclable (the paper in this book already has been). It's a good thing to produce compost that will nurture a tree's growth; it's even better not to cut the tree down. If your community has a curbside collection program, you really ought to give it whatever types of waste paper it will take.

These will most likely be newsprint and office paper—and unfortunately, the kinds of paper that remain are those least suited to composting. Glossy papers are coated with clays and that makes the fibers resistant to water and so resistant to decomposition as well. The colored inks splashed across the brochures and sweepstakes entry forms may contain heavy metals (not all publishers are as careful to use nontoxic inks as we have been). Equally bad are the papers that have been whitened with bleaches—they will likely contain dioxins and formaldehyde.

If your community doesn't recycle newspaper, perhaps you should consider adding it to your heap. Before you do, though, you should call the publisher and find out if the news is printed with soy- or petroleum-based inks (we've used soy-based inks to print this book). Petroleum-based inks will contribute something called *polycyclic aromatic hydrocarbons* to your heap, and although a thorough composting should decompose all but 2 or 3 percent of these, any that remain may act as carcinogens. Not worth the risk, in our opinion.

Having said all this, we should note that waste paper is playing an increasingly prominent role in the composting business. Farmers are finding that when shredded fine it makes an excellent bedding for cattle and poultry. Farmer Ronald G. Webb of Gardiner, Maine, for example, has found old telephone directories to be even more absorbent than hay or sawdust, and cleaner, too, so that udder infections among his 130-head dairy herd have significantly declined, as have the bacterial levels in his milk. He's taking six tons of directories off New England Telephone's hands every week and after spreading them in the barn he mixes them with food scraps from a local supermarket chain and turns the whole mess into free fertilizer.

That saves money for both the farmer and the phone company. But the most intriguing case of paper composting we ever heard of cost billions—literally. A ·

couple of years ago we came across a brief report in *The Wall Street Journal* about the German government's proposal to compost 2 million pounds of communist banknotes that it had inherited with the reunification of the country. We have never been able to find out what came of this, though we somehow can't imagine Teutonic bankers agreeing to such a sacrilegious treatment of their stock in trade. But if they did, what those pin-striped composters produced was "black gold" indeed.

Politically Correct Diapers

The hullabaloo seems to have died away now, but remember a couple of years ago when the disposable versus cloth diaper debate still raged? As a parent, Tom misses it, if only because those heated discussions provided some relief from the utter boredom of Lamaze classes.

In between helping his wife Suzanne learn how to breathe (you would think she'd have that down by age 38), Tom would listen in on the crescendo of charges and countercharges. At that time (1989), the cotton diaper faction was on the attack. Pointing fingers at disposable-diaper-using (former) friends, the cotton users would charge them with placing convenience before the health of the environment. All those trees pulped (1,000,265,000 tons every year), all those petrochemicals (75,000 metric tons), just so *you* don't have to clean up after your kid. Disposable diaper users would reply by quoting studies indicating that growing, bleaching, and weaving the cotton for reusables actually consumed more resources than keeping a baby furnished with disposables. *You*, they would add, pointing back at the cotton crowd—are a terrible burden on the sewage treatment system.

Tom decided to get to the bottom of this matter, which was a big mistake. Each side kept bringing in scientific gunslingers, and Tom would no sooner finish one study than he would come across another that would completely contradict the first. In the end, he could only find one point on which all sides seemed to agree: disposable diapers contributed as much as 1.8 percent (by volume) of what went to the landfill. That seemed like a lot. So Tom and Suzanne laid in a mountain of unbleached cotton diapers.

But maybe they should have thrown their support to the disposables. Thanks to Procter & Gamble (the major player in this industry), disposable diapers are promising to become what composting mavens refer to as "an organic resource." P&G funded an experiment at a Minnesota composting plant in which soiled disposable diapers were composted along with mixed municipal waste. First they added diapers at a rate of 2 percent, the rate at which they occur in the average waste stream. Then the researchers "enriched" the waste stream, bringing the total volume of diapers to 4 percent. Then 8 percent.

In every case the diapers composted completely, and the end-product met all the EPA standards for pathogens. In other words, the finished compost was clean and safe, or at least, any problems with the finished product were due to other household wastes such as batteries and cosmetics that we discard without a second thought (and no one was yelling about those things at Lamaze class).

The diapers did introduce one nontoxic contaminant into the finished compost—the diapers' plastic coversheets. In the Minnesota study, this material was removed by screening the finished compost. A Procter & Gamble spokesman told us, however, that the company was already (as of 1993) test-marketing a disposable with a completely compostable cover. He couldn't reveal the exact formula, but he assured us that this cover was not made of so-called compostable plastic, and that normal handling in a normal composting plant would reduce it to CO_2, water, and mineral end-products—that is, it would become true compost. He also pointed out that diaper composting is already a reality. Every municipal composting plant that processes mixed solid waste includes disposable diapers as a matter of course.

Tom never did figure out all the position papers, so we aren't going to recommend one kind of diaper or another. His experience was that disposables clearly had convenience on their side, but that the cotton diapers brought him close to his child in a way he would not otherwise have experienced. For what that was worth. Besides, the cotton diapers make great rags now that Matthew is toilet trained. When they wear out, Tom plans to compost them. That's one more advantage of the cotton reusables—they are a bioresource you don't have to give away.

TNT at LAAP and BAAP

We've tried hard throughout this chapter to keep it relevant to your situation; but we can't bear to close it without some reference to the strangest compostable we've ever encountered. We only hope that you won't ever have to use this know-how.

You think recycling is a pain—all that time spent scrubbing out cans and ripping little cellophane windows out of the envelopes that arrive with bills you don't want to get anyway? It could be worse. You could be the U.S. Army, which in the course of recycling munitions at its stockpiles here and there around the country (such as at LAAP—the Louisiana Army Ammunition

Plant—or at BAAP in Badger, Wisconsin) has contaminated thousands of tons of soil.

Clean out all those unreliable, overage old shells and what do you do with the pink wash water? You run it out to lagoons and let it evaporate, and it's gone. But the soil underneath ends up *full* of TNT. Which can cause gastrointestinal disturbance should it find its way into your drinking water, or toxic hepatitis, delirium convulsions, and coma.

The proper name for this explosive is *Trinitrotoluene,* according to our encyclopedia, and that weighty volume included a diagram of the chemical structure that showed a ring of carbon, nitrogen, oxygen, and hydrogen. If you read the introduction to this chapter, that should set you thinking. It apparently rang a few bells with waste disposal specialists hired by the Army, because they realized that TNT and its derivatives RDX and HMX are organic and decided to try composting them. The waste people called Woods End Research Laboratory (WERL), which in turn developed a special composting formula for use in a pilot project at a Umatilla, Oregon, facility known to the brass as UMDA (Umatilla Army Depot Activity).

The object was to keep the pile hot as long as possible, since the TNT breakdown proceeded most quickly at thermophilic temperatures. Woods End developed a formula that, as usual, made use of locally abundant ingredients, most notably the wastes from a vegetable-processing plant and buffalo chips from a nearby ranch. This was one instance where the composters really wanted to get the mix right the first time, especially in calculating the quantity of explosive-laced soil. Boost the TNT content over 12 percent, and the contamination problem may solve itself in a most spectacular way.

In the event, the Woods End recipe tested long-burning but nonexplosive, and effective, ultimately reducing the TNT by 97 percent or so. Actually, the TNT has proved susceptible to a number of other mixes, compost formulas that include alfalfa, horse feed, apple pomace, sawdust, potato waste, and, of course, horse and chicken manure (or HM and CM as those acronymists at the Pentagon call them—and lord knows they're experts on both). The Army actually adopted this method for cleansing several AAPs—which is astonishing, because it costs half as much as incineration, the alternative, and could end up saving taxpayers several hundred million dollars. A peace dividend at last?

CHAPTER 6

Getting Started

COMPOST HAPPENS. That may sound like a euphemistic bumper sticker, but it's the truth.[1] It's what you should keep in mind, too, as you try to put together your own heap. Composting is easy. It's a very forgiving process.

You'd never guess that, though, to listen to the experts. For them, composting is a cult. They worship the stuff their heaps and bins and gizmos produce — "black gold" is what they generally call it — and if you believe

---

[1] In fact, after writing this, I discovered that it *is* the text of a bumper sticker. And of a button, too. I have one — it was a gift from Will Brinton of Woods End Research Laboratory who developed this as his company slogan more than a year ago. I agreed to give him credit, O.K., but if he ever wants to sell a biodegradable bumper sticker ("Compost This Sticker") he's going to have to credit *us*.

them, it will fix anything but the federal deficit. But—
and this is crucial—compost only works if you make it
their way. That involves an elaborate ritual of steps, recipes, and apparatus, and what's more, the ritual is different for every single compost priest or priestess. Stray
an inch from the path of biodegradable righteousness,
and you risk (according to them) excommunication
and, worse, a god-awful stink.

If you find yourself cornered by one of these compost cultists, don't resist. Remember, there's no point in
arguing with a fanatic. Smile, nod a lot, sift a little bit
of the black gold through your fingers, and agree that
it is great stuff. It probably is. Then go home and compost your own way.

For those who don't yet have their own method of
composting, what follows is a series of suggestions.
These are not rules, just insights Marty and Tom have
gathered over months and years of decay. They should
be enough to enable you to develop your own routines.

These may take any of a number of forms. There is,
for example, the off-the-cuff method at one time es-
poused by Marty. Before he met Tom and began his ca-
reer as a serious composter, Marty had already achieved
some success with what Tom calls the "Uriah Heap"—
it was *very* humble. Any aggregation of organic waste
Marty was liable to declare a compost heap. The result
was a low, shabby, amorphous mound. But under the
thatch of old leaves and twigs, eventually you would
find a core of black, crumbly COMPOST!

There's not much to boast about in that style of
composting (at least not in Tom's compulsive opinion)
but it does work, after a fashion. It is slow—the un-
tended heap may take two or more years to decompose
fully. It's inefficient, too, because the rain washes most
of the nutrients out of the heap before the organic matter has finished turning into humus. Quality control is

about like that of a Yugo factory; there's no plan to what goes into the heap, so there's no telling what sort of humus this method will produce. It can produce sizable quantities of usable compost, though, and the investment of time and energy certainly is low.

As Marty would be the first to admit, there are lots more effective methods of composting. We could present you with a recipe—and will, at the end of this chapter, where you will find profiles of three classic methods of composting. But first we are going to help you design your own method. After all, everybody's garbage is different, and so is their situation. Customizing your compost ("Kustom Kompost") is easy. All you have to do is keep in mind the following points:

1. *Location.* Where you put your heap will go far to determining the success of this venture. It has to be accessible, both for loading and unloading, or you will abandon composting as a nuisance. Don't put it so far down a muddy path that taking out the garbage becomes a cross-country hike; if you do, the vegetable peelings and stale bread will pile up in the kitchen sink until the decomposers move in there. Make sure, too, that the heap is accessible to wheelbarrow or garden cart so that you don't have to hump the finished compost out to lawn or garden in baskets on your head.

How you feel about your heap will also influence where you put it. There are two basic schools of composters—those who (like Tom and Marty) consider a heap intrinsically unsightly and like to hide it, and those more earthy types who want this alchemical device out on display. Both Tom and Marty have stashed their composters behind the garage where neither they nor the neighbors have to look at it. But what if your yard offers no hiding places, or if you want to come out of the closet with your composting? There's no reason why a neatly constructed wooden bin must be an eyesore, and those rotating drum type composters make every bit as good a garden ornament as a pink flamingo or gnome. With a little ingenuity, you might even be able to disguise it as a truck tire planted with petunias.

2. *Feeding the heap.* Compost cultists fuss more over their heaps' diets than their own. There is some reason for this. Even if all the things you add to the heap are compostable, if you gorge it with too much of one kind of waste, you may cause the composting to go wrong. What's the worst-case scenario? A meltdown that smells like a particularly fresh manure pile. But it's genuinely difficult to achieve this —you have to really work at it— and if you keep in mind one basic rule, you will steer clear of trouble.

To give your heap a balanced meal, you must maintain the proper ratio of carbon to nitrogen. That sounds complicated, but it isn't. Both these elements are essential building blocks for plant growth. Carbon as we have already pointed out is the *sine qua non* of every organic molecule, so anything biological needs lots of that, while nitrogen is a small but key part of amino acids and proteins. Feed the heap too much carbon and decomposition slows to a stagger, since carbon (which mostly comes from woody tissue, cellulose) is hard to digest. Feed the heap too much nitrogen and you get your stink, since the nitrogen starts escaping as NH_3— gaseous ammonia.

What is the right balance of carbon to nitrogen? Scientists have determined that the ideal ratio is somewhere around 25 or 30 to 1 (25:1–30:1); that is, the materials you add to the heap should contain about twenty-five to thirty times as much carbon as nitrogen. Very few materials, by themselves, offer that. Sawdust, for example, tests out somewhere between 200:1 and 750:1 while grass clippings run about 12–25:1 and vegetable scraps run 12–20:1. Timothy hay actually comes in at 25:1, right on the nose. So does that mean that the ideal compost heap would contain nothing but timothy hay? Of course not. It means that your heap should contain a blend of high-carbon and high-nitrogen materials. It should be, in short, a compromise.

If this mathematical jargon is making you nervous, relax. For the benefit of those who are comfortable with number-crunching, we are including a table of the carbon and nitrogen contents of various compostables. With this the mathematically gifted can calculate exactly how much dry leaves they should add to the heap to temper the bushel of fresh grass clippings they just added. Their reward will be a more rapid decomposition. But for the rest of us, there is no need to take the computer out to the heap. Composting, as we have already noted, is a forgiving process, and a very rough and ready compromise is enough to keep the decomposers happy.

Our number-free solution is to divide materials into two classes: green and juicy versus dry and brown. Green and juicy compostables are materials such as vegetable peelings (say, 12:1), grass clippings (an average of 19:1), or fresh cow manure (20:1–and if you don't think this qualifies as green and juicy, you've never worked on a dairy farm). Examples of brown compostables are dry leaves (30–80:1), sawdust (200–750:1), or straw (40–100:1). We start by mixing these things about two to one (two parts brown to one part green), and then check the heap periodically.

If it starts subsiding into a gooey mess, we stir in some of the dry leaves from the bag-full we keep by the bin. If the heap cools off, and the dry browns seem to be just sitting there, we might add some more green and juicies. We should add, too, that not all nitrogen sources are green and juicy. Virtually every animal manure is a good source of nitrogen, even those that, like

Carbon vs. nitrogen — a balanced diet for your heap*

Decomposers need both carbon and nitrogen and perform best if given these materials in something like a 25 to 1 or 30 to 1 ratio. That is, the compostables should contain twenty-five to thirty times as much carbon as nitrogen. Compost mavens tend to make a big deal out of this, offering elaborate arithmetical formulas that disciples are supposed to use in measuring out a little of this and a little of that, to ensure that the final blend is just so. We can't be bothered. But it's worth knowing something about the carbon to nitrogen ratios (C:N) of common compostables since choking the heap with one element or the other will cause problems. Loading the heap up with carbon while starving it of nitrogen will slow decomposition to a glacial creep, and loading it up with nitrogen while starving it of carbon may create an awful stink. So check below, and if you find that your favorite compostable has a high nitrogen value, find something in the high carbon column that you can blend with it.

Commonly available, nitrogen-rich compostables	C:N ratio
Poultry manure (fresh)	10:1
Poultry manure (with bedding)	13–18:1
Vegetable wastes	12–20:1
Seaweed	17:1
Grass clippings	12–25:1
Coffee grounds (the writer's special)	20:1
Cow manure	20:1
Hay (your average bale)	15–32:1
Horse manure	25:1
Water hyacinth — fresh (for Floridians)	20–30:1

Commonly available, carbon-rich compostables	
Horse manure with bedding (straw or wood shavings)	30–60:1
Leaves	30–80:1
Shrub trimmings	53:1
Tree trimmings	70:1
Straw	40–100:1

Bark	100–130:1
Paper	150–200:1
Sawdust	200–750:1
Woodchips, shavings, etc., from hardwood trees	560:1
Corrugated cardboard	563:1
Newsprint	398–852:1
Woodchips, shavings, etc., from softwood trees	641:1
Telephone books	772:1

Uncommon (but who knows?) and nitrogen rich

Fish wastes	3.6:1
Shrimp wastes	3.4:1
Crab and lobster wastes	4.9:1
Poultry carcasses	5:1
Pig manure	14:1
Horse manure from the race track	41:1
Sheep manure	16:1
Turkey litter	16:1

Uncommon and carbon rich

Corn stalks	60:1
Lumbermill waste	170:1

*C:N figures taken from *On-Farm Composting Handbook* and *Composting to Reduce the Waste Stream*, publications of the Northeast Regional Agricultural Engineering Service: Ithaca, NY.

horse apples, are brown or that, like chicken manure, are distinctly unjuicy. You can resort to the various kinds of nitrogen fertilizers down at the garden center. Tom has even emptied into his heap the bucket of ammonia water left over from mopping the kitchen floor.

Manures are a natural for the compost heap, and horse owners in particular are grateful, usually, to anyone who hauls the stuff away. But composting synthetic nitrogen seems to us not only unnecessary but also environmentally irresponsible. Anyway, it runs counter to the self-reliant spirit of composting. Since we don't need to turn out finished compost in two weeks (and with the right C:N ratio, that can be done), generally we add a few more vegetable scraps or the wormy apples from the backyard tree if the composting seems to be lagging. Then we let nature take its course.

3. *Watering the heap.* Water is also necessary to the composting process. Just like you and me, microorganisms are mostly composed of water and they need a moist environment if they are to reproduce. Green and juicies supply some moisture, but almost always it's necessary to water the heap, too, as you build it and periodically thereafter. Remember as you do so that the decomposers you want are the aerobic ones—that is, the ones that need oxygen to survive. Keep the heap soaking wet, and you'll drown them. So instead, aim to keep the heap evenly moist, about like a sponge after you've wetted it and then squeezed it lightly.

If you are feeling lazy, or maybe just thrifty, you can also moisten the heap by leaving it uncovered through the occasional rainstorm. Don't leave it uncovered all the time, though, at least not if you live in a region with a rainy climate. Too much rainwater will turn the heap soggy, and it will also wash most of the nutrients out of your compost. That's why we recommend keeping your bin or heap covered. Tom (typically) has built a wood and fiberglass cover for his bin, but you can achieve the same protection by draping a couple of old plastic bags over the top of your heap. By the way, if you do over-water your compost heap, through a too-enthusiastic use of the hose or by leaving it open to a real deluge, you can easily correct the contents' overmoistened condition by stirring in some more browns.

4. *Aerating the heap.* Air is as essential as water to healthy compost. That's because the decomposers you want in your heap are mostly aerobic—that is, they need oxygen to flourish. Bacteria, fungi, and bugs that find a niche at the outside of the heap have access to all the oxygen they want; at least they will unless you have made the mistake of enclosing your heap in some bin that impedes the flow of air around the heap. In any case, the decomposers in the interior of the heap don't have direct access to atmospheric oxygen—they must depend on the little pockets of air that lurk between the bits of compostables. This is especially unfortunate since it is the interior decomposers who have the greatest need for air. After all, in a thermophilic or mesophilic heap, the decomposers in the heap's warm heart are the ones who do most of the work. That's why it's important to keep the heap as fluffy as possible.

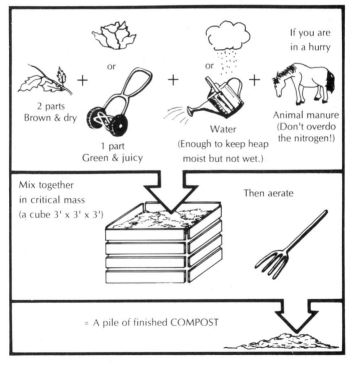

FIGURE 9. Composting made even easier: a schematic recipe to pin to the side of your bin.

Above all, don't tamp the compostables down as you add them. Old-time guides to composting used to recommend this, and it does indeed allow you to pack more waste into a heap. Besides, it seems neater somehow. But its effect will be to smother the decomposers.

Unfortunately, no matter how fluffy you leave your heap, the decomposers will consume the oxygen it contains within a few weeks—maybe much faster if the heap really starts to cook. You'll know this is happening when the compost suddenly and mysteriously cools. Decomposition has been booming along, steam comes pouring out every time you poke the heap, and then one morning: nothing. You find the heap that only yesterday could cook a chicken (see Chapter 8 for the recipe), but now it's like a bowl of soup that was too long on the way from the stove to the table. Tepid. And pretty soon it's ice cold.

If you don't do anything at this point, the heap will continue to decompose, but only very gradually. Composting may take a year or more to complete. But once again, the remedy is simple. Just aerate the heap.

There are a couple of ways to do that. The most efficient is to fluff the heap, stirring it up with a pitchfork. Tom has built himself a compost bin that consists of three compartments that sit side by side. He loads the first one; then when the heap inside it cools, he forks the compostables into the next compartment. Twenty minutes of moderate work is all this takes. Then, a few weeks later, he forks the heap from the second compartment to the third. That's all the turning his heap needs to complete its composting within a couple of months.

If your bin only offers a single compartment or if you don't feel up to the labor of turning your heap, you can also aerate it by sticking a fork into it and tossing it like a salad. This, of course, is the virtue of one of the drum composters that looks like a barrel mounted on an axle. Even when fully loaded the drum is relatively easy to turn, and a few rotations each day or so is enough to remix the contents and keep them well aerated.

If you don't want to spring for the drum composter and yet really hate the idea of any exercise; if, in short, you feel that sweat should only happen in a health club; you can build an aerating system into the heap as you assemble it. To do this you'll have to spend some money on plastic pipe and tools, but not much, maybe $15. In an optimistic moment, Tom did this.

He went to the local builder's supply and bought a couple of lengths of flexible 6-inch plastic drainage pipe. Then, after hauling them home in his Japanese subcompact (it was like riding in a carton full of snakes) Tom cut them into 3-foot sections with a wood saw. That took maybe 15 minutes. Then he invested another 45 minutes perforating the pipe walls with an electric drill and a ½-inch wood bit.

The following afternoon, as he filled one of his bin's compartments with a mixture of horse manure (that's juicy, even if not exactly green, with a 15–25:1 ratio) and shredded leaves (50:1), he stopped every so often to insert a leaky pipe across the bin — once buried, these served as channels to bring air into the heap's interior. Altogether he worked nine pipes into a 3 × 3 × 3-foot pile.

A problem soon emerged: as the adjacent bin (which Tom had filled with an unventilated pile of the same manure-leaf mix) heated up to 150°F, the ventilated one stayed cool. Even after Tom boosted its nitrogen content by digging in a bushel of sappy, sugary apple pulp left over from cider making, it never warmed past the mesophilic stage. Holding his hand next to the end of one of his pipe ventilators, Tom could feel the heat escaping—while supplying oxygen, the ventilators were also working as a cooling system.

Which only proves what Tom's Yankee father always insisted—that there's no substitute for a bit of hard work (especially if it is someone else's).

5. *Critical mass.* The failure of Tom's ventilation system highlights one more important factor in the success of your composting system. If you want the compost to heat to 150°F, the temperature that kills weed seeds and pathogens, then you need a certain minimum mass of materials. In a large heap, the outer material acts as insulation, retaining the heat the decomposers produce and keeping the heap's interior a hospitable environment for the thermophiles. (Of course, if you want that outer material to compost, too, then you must turn it into the center when you aerate the heap with your pitchfork.) To provide adequate insulation for high-temperature decomposition, you need at least a cubic yard of compostables.

It would seem that if a cubic yard is good, then a heap with a volume of 2 cubic yards, 5 cubic yards, or even 25 cubic yards would be better. But too large a heap is too difficult to aerate, and even the commercial composters, who turn their materials with machines, prefer to lay them out in long, thin windrows.

What if your household doesn't produce enough waste to fill a 3 × 3 × 3-foot bin? You can gather organic wastes from around the neighborhood as Tom does, picking up the leaves that the neighbors rake into piles on the curb, and stopping by the riding school to share windfall apples (the ones you don't compost) with the horses and take home a trash can full of their manure in return.

If scavenging doesn't appeal to you, that's OK, too. You can compost with less than this critical mass. You just have to be a bit more patient, and you should give a little more attention to what you add to the heap. Take extra care not to add any weeds that have gone to seed. Your cooler composting won't cook the seeds like a hot heap would, and a few months or years of burial won't bother the weed seeds one bit—they can survive decades or even centuries of burial to sprout normally as soon as they are returned to the soil surface. For the same reason, make sure to add only healthy plant materials to your cooler heap. Toss an aphid-covered broccoli seedling into a big, high-temperature heap and the heat will kill the bugs; add the same scrap of refuse to your small low-temperature heap and you'll fill it full of bug-eggs that may survive to start an epidemic in next year's compost-enriched vegetable patch.

6. *Bin or heap?* There are composters who prefer to pile their compostables in free-standing heaps. And then there are those (like Tom) who prefer a bin. In truth, it doesn't much matter which approach you take, as long as you make sure that the mass of compostables is exposed to the air (solid wood or plastic bins are not a good idea) and protected from the rain and snow.

The principal advantage of a bin is that it's easier to keep tidy. A trim pile of neatly stacked manure, leaves, and other vegetable wastes can look just fine, but it takes a bit of extra care to build and maintain it that way. To feed a bin, you simply lift the lid or open the hatch and toss the stuff in. Then it disappears from sight.

There are lots of designs for do-it-yourself bins floating around, and we've included illustrations of a couple with this chapter. A 4-foot-wide cylinder of wire mesh works as well as anything else; another easy and effective solution is to lash four old loading pallets together into a bottomless box.

You can get much fancier than this. Tom spent a whole weekend and more than $100 constructing the three-compartment bin. He used durable materials (pressure-treated lumber and heavy galvanized mesh), so the investment will probably turn out to be a good one. But a Cadillac composter like this is not only unnecessary, it's also a sign that compost may be assuming too central a role in your life.

With gardening becoming the favorite hobby of what were once called *yuppies* (most of them seem to have had children and moved to the suburbs, which makes them something unpronounceable), slick, *engineered* bins are coming increasingly into fashion. Many of these do work (we'll look at a few of these in the next chapter, too). If you've got the cash, and your self-esteem depends on driving the ultimate composting machine, well, be our guest. The end result will be the same — humus — and how you get there isn't important.

7. *To shred or not to shred.* Shredding the compostables before you add them to the heap is a practice recommended by almost every veteran composter. The benefit is twofold. Shredding increases the surface area of the materials you add to the heap, thus increasing the area of compost that the decomposers can attack. Besides, most plant parts, whether leaves, stems, roots, or fruits, are enclosed in skins that are designed to resist the entry of fungi and bacteria. These skins make quite an effective barrier and, if left intact, they can delay decay by weeks or months.

Tom (who hates red Delicious apples and yet inherited a tree of that variety when he bought his present house) has bushels of apples to dispose of every fall. He has found that a crushed or chopped apple disappears within days of being dug into a heap of hot compost; a whole apple remains recognizable for a month or more. The leaves he rakes up in the fall are the mainstay of his composting; if left whole, these mat down into wet, airless lumps and may take a couple of years to compost.

When shredded, they stay as light as confetti and break down in a couple of months.

If you want to compost at high temperatures, you'll find it helpful to shred the material you use to build the heap. In addition, a really good shredder (and we'll discuss the hallmarks of these in Chapter 7) will make available all sorts of additional wastes. Tree branches or brush take years to rot on their own. If chipped, they too will compost in weeks or at most months.

Marty, with his inexhaustible fund of patience, has elected not to shred; Tom has taken a low-tech (i.e., cheap) approach. Whoever is cooking in his house roughly chops the vegetable scraps before dumping them into the for-the-composter container. For several seasons, he made do by using his lawnmower to shred the leaves (see Chapter 7 for a description of that). But he finally broke down (or, to be more accurate, the mower broke down), and he bought an electric leaf shredder.

This is nothing more than a string trimmer mounted below a giant funnel. It costs less than $100, it's maintenance free, and it reduces a large bag of leaves to confetti in five minutes. It won't shred anything else, though. Tom has tried feeding it plant stalks, grass clippings, etc., and they only jammed the machine's nylon jaws. There are plenty of more powerful chipper-shredders available, machines that can handle almost anything you throw their way, but our reaction to those is mixed. For a brief and idiosyncratic guide, once again look to Chapter 7.

8. *Ripening.* We have already mentioned the problem involved in the use of immature compost. If the organic materials are not completely decomposed when you dig them into your garden bed, they will finish the process in the soil, and the decomposers may steal the nitrates they find there. The nitrates will be returned with interest when composting finishes, but in the meantime your plants may suffer from a temporary nutrient deficiency.

There's an easy cure for that: replace what the decomposers take by sprinkling the bed with a nitrogen-rich fertilizer. Personally, we feel this defeats the purpose of composting, which for us is to reduce the unnecessary consumption of natural resources. But many gardeners disagree, and they prefer to do all their composting by digging materials into the soil absolutely fresh and letting them compost entirely *in situ.* This is called "sheet composting," since the compostables are typically spread in a sheet over the surface of the bed and then rototilled in. It will boost the organic content of the soil, but unless you are willing to leave the bed fallow until the compostables have decomposed completely, you will have to resort to extra fertilization.

We prefer patience to fertilizer, and we make sure that decomposition is complete before we remove the compost from its bin. To do this we wait until the heap has cooled, and the compostables have settled into a mass of indistinguishable particles. Then we allow the compost to ripen another four to eight weeks, to give the organic matter time to finish its transformation to humus. Only after this do we hand it over to the plants.

Three Classic Recipes

Having read the eight pointers on the preceding pages, you have all the information you need to start composting yourself. Novices, however, may appreciate a model on which to base their first effort, and for their benefit the following pages include a look at three classic methods. Veteran composters have already worked out routines that suit them. Still, they hopefully will appreciate the material that comes next in the same way that a wine connoisseur savors visits to great wineries. Along the way, they may pick up a few tips, too, that will improve their own homebrew.

The Indore Process

This is what Sir Albert Howard called the composting system he developed during his quarter century as an agricultural adviser in central India (1905–1931). Howard was the first great apostle of organic gardening, and his work remains the foundation of this movement.

One reason that Howard's work attracted so much attention at the time was his thoroughly respectable, conventional credentials: he was a university-trained, scientific agriculturist who came to believe that improving crop yields would require a holistic approach. Instead of addressing such matters as soil fertility or pest control piecemeal, and treating each symptom of a problem separately, Howard realized that the soil and crop—and the farmer, too—must be treated as a single system. This led to his emphasis on healthy, biologically active soil, and his discovery of the fundamental role that humus plays in creating and maintaining this condition. His study of soil microorganisms, then a new field, led to an interest in microbial decomposers and from there to a revolutionary understanding of composting.

He began to see managed decomposition as the means to what had become a cherished goal: Howard was determined to devise a way in which average rural Indians could replenish their fields' humus supply. In 1924 the Darbar of the central Indian state of Indore helped him found his own agricultural research institute. There, over the next seven years, Howard developed the first scientifically based composting system.

To make this process practical for the primitive farmers it was supposed to serve, Howard kept it simple and made sure it didn't depend on sophisticated chemistry or machinery. An incidental effect of this was to make his composting attractive to weekend gardeners as well. The ironic result was that though composting never caught on in India to the extent Howard had hoped—that nation has preferred to pursue the "green revolution" of agricultural chemists—it has revolutionized the way that educated Westerners understand agriculture.

As adapted by American J. I. Rodale, the Indore Process soon became the central rite of the U.S. organic gardening movement. In the at-times-dogmatic hands of organic gardeners, this composting method has restored thousands of acres of exhausted soil and made the suburbs bloom like the rose.

What is the Indore Process? As originally designed by Howard, it required a supply of manure, and ideally this should be mixed with the urine-soaked bedding from the stalls. That is what I pick up at the stable, but Howard to the contrary, this material isn't essential. Rodale and his followers have proven that virtually any source of organic nitrogen can substitute for manure if none is readily available.

Howard did his composting in pits, but that was because Indore is a dry region and enclosure in a pit protected the compostables from dehydration. In the rainier regions, he recommended building the heap above ground and that is what American disciples generally do.

Classically, you make such a heap at least 5 feet long and 5 feet wide—Howard measured his materials in ox-cart loads—and you begin it with a layer of brush—this helps ventilate the heap by allowing some air to penetrate through its bottom. On top of this you spread a 6-inch-thick layer of vegetable waste, and on top of this you lay 2 inches of manure, the fresher the better. Cap this with a layer of soil perhaps ⅛ inch thick (this introduces into the heap the decomposers found naturally in the soil) and a sprinkling of pulverized limestone (this is to prevent an acid condition from developing within the heap—the decomposers prefer an environment that is pH neutral, neither acidic nor alkaline). Moisten all the materials thoroughly and begin again, adding layers of green stuff, manure, and soil in sequence until the heap reaches a height of 5 feet.

As with Tom's heap (which is loosely modeled on an Indore heap), you let the heap heat up, then as soon as it starts to cool, turn it over with a pitchfork. This mixes the materials and aerates them, and you moisten the heap once again (if necessary) as you rebuild it. The heap should heat up again; when it cools again, you turn it a second time. Howard's enormous heaps (for farm use, he recommended building them 30 × 14 × 3 feet deep) completed their composting in about three months. Depending on the heat of the season and the care you take in managing it, your home heap should mature in half that time. At that point, as Albert Howard pronounced in his book, *The Soil and Health,* your Indore heap "will have fulfilled its purpose—the restitution of their manurial rights to the soils of this planet."[2]

Cosmic Compost

Howard's goal was to fill bellies; but he had a contemporary who promoted composting as a means of feeding the soul. This was Rudolf Steiner, an Austrian philosopher and educator who is best remembered today for attaching polygraphs to his house plants (he

---

[2]Sir Albert Howard, *The Soil and Health* (New York: Devin-Adair, 1947), p. 52.

used this machine to prove that they responded to his greetings, lectures, threats, etc.). I knew only of this work, and had dismissed him as a crackpot until I learned that Steiner was the pioneer of biodynamic agriculture.

This was the philosophy that would inspire Alan Chadwick and John Jeavons, two leading lights of California's ecology movement in the 1970s and 1980s. I've seen in a variety of gardens the spectacular results biodynamics can produce, and I admire its beneficial effect on the environment; unlike conventional horticulture, it does not turn the garden into a sink for resources, but instead promotes the garden as a self-sufficient source of renewal to the land around. As practiced by Steiner, biodynamics was also a source of renewal to gardeners. He believed it could be a way for man to rediscover the spiritual wisdom of the ancients and reintegrate himself with nature. Biodynamics restores the soil—and it is intended to restore as well that dreamlike consciousness man once possessed but that through a devotion to materialism he had lost.

At least I think that's what it is. After attending a harvest festival at one of Steiner's schools in Spring Valley, New York (nice—lots of parents folk-dancing with stumbling toddlers, good musicians, good food, and a special composting information booth), I walked down the road to what had been the associated farm (a victim of suburban sprawl) and at the surviving bookstore bought a book: *Culture and Horticulture: A Philosophy of Gardening,* by Wolf D. Storl.[3] I've been puzzling away at that ever since, with mixed results.

I can't quite follow all the references to Aristotle and Paracelsus, alchemy, and aborigines. I don't intend

---

[3](Wyoming, RI: Biodynamic Literature, 1979).

to start practicing astrological gopher control, either, or use quartz crystals to focus cosmic energy. That's not my style. Here and there, though, throughout this book, statements of startling good sense leap out from the page.

"Nature can be seen as man exteriorized, and man as nature interiorized." Hmmm. "Low productivity, insects and disease are not the problem, they are the symptoms. Spraying bugs ground up in a blender, using trichogramma wasps, etc. is treating the symptom, whereas building the soil and one's relationship to the land is treating the problem." Absolutely.

Composting is central to rebuilding a relationship to the land. Compost, according to Steiner, is full of vital energies. As Steiner's amanuensis Storl put it, composting is "bio-dynamics par excellence, for here one is neither letting nature take its course, nor is one violating nature's principles, but one is aiding nature, speeding her up a bit, and guiding the changes in such a way that it is beneficial for the garden organism." Giving the old girl a goose, as it were.

Managing the heap wasn't haphazard in the communities his followers founded — it was serious business to be supervised by the Kompostmeister. He or she made sure that the ingredients contained the proper rations of carbon to nitrogen and piled the material into windrows 4 feet high, 6 feet wide, "and as long as necessary" to ensure the critical mass essential to the biochemical processes. The Kompostmeister bedded the heap on straw or some other absorptive substance so that any liquid runoff would be saved, along with the nutrients it contained, and coated the pile with a skin of peat, sawdust, or straw to make sure that the ammonia generated during decay was trapped and recycled (Steiner agreed with Bill Bricker the Kricket King that a stink betrayed a loss of goodness).

So far, all was rational. But Steiner also promoted the use of inoculants — compost starters — whose ingredients defy conventional science. Initially, the recipes were closely guarded by the Anthroposophical Society he founded, and initiates were sworn not to reveal them to outsiders. But, in the best journalistic tradition, the book I purchased told all.

Steiner believed that certain preparations would regulate the chemistry of the compost and make it especially receptive to the workings of the planets. For this he used herbs: chamomile, yarrow, dandelion, stinging nettle, oak bark, and valerian. All are favorites of the old-time herbalists, and Steiner's reasoning, apparently, was that the same astrological and chemical properties that made these herbs healing to man would apply to microorganisms. Think of them as digestives for the decomposers. Their manufacture is also a part of the gardener developing a personal relationship to his or her own garden, so homebrews are preferred to off-the-shelf versions.

Most, alas, involve packing herbs into the body parts of slaughtered animals — a cow's horn, a sheep's skull, or the bladder of a stag — and then burying them in the soil for some months. Afterward, they are added in minute amounts (a teaspoon per 3 cubic yards of composting material) in a deep hole poked into the top of the heap.

The problem I face in taking this last step to genuine anthroposophical compost is obvious. In Connecticut, land of relentlessly awful Yankee cuisine, I cannot find a butcher I trust to supply a decent roast, let alone a stag's bladder. But in my by now well-thumbed guide to biodynamics, there is a disapproving reference to a short cut.[4] A renegade British anthroposophist, a Miss

---

[4]Storl, p. 361.

Maye Bruce, distilled Steiner's instructions into what she called "Quick-Return Composting." A trip to the New York Botanical Garden Library turned up *her* book (*Quick-Return Composting*), complete with the revelation that came to her in a dream — "The Divinity within the flower is sufficient of Itself" — and recipes almost as easy as Minute Rice.

Gather flowers of chamomile, dandelion, valerian, yarrow, and stinging nettle before midsummer, moisten them with rainwater, and crush them (each type of flower in a separate batch) with a mortar and pestle. Wrap the mess in muslin, and press out the resulting juices. Pass them through filter paper until absolutely clear. At the same time, steep one teaspoonful of powdered oak bark in 2 ounces of rainwater, stir well, let sit for 24 hours, then strain. Combine all these essences with rainwater at a rate of one drop each per ounce, mix with equal parts honey, then further dilute with rainwater at a rate of 2 teaspoonfuls of essences per pint. The result will be enough inoculant to energize a normal cubic-yard compost heap.

Capitalist Compost

As a horticulturalist and former resident of Hoboken, New Jersey, Tom always looked up to Peter Henderson. Henderson was a Scottish immigrant who came to the United States in 1843; he settled in Jersey, down by Exit 14, establishing a market garden a mile or two from the future site of Tom's apartment. Within a few years, Henderson had become famous for the ferryloads of vegetables, fruits, and flowers he was sending to Manhattan.

The secret of his green thumb was blisters. Although Henderson advocated gardening as the best therapy for invalids, he also warned anyone considering it as a profession that they must be up to fourteen hours of hard, physical labor a day. EVERY DAY. Tom has spoken to Henderson's great-granddaughter, who admitted that not even her grandmother had any clear memories of Henderson since he always left home before dawn and returned only after dark.

Henderson had a second secret, too, though. Possessed of the true Scot's thrift, he figured out a way to tap into what was then New Jersey's most abundant resource: garbage! Things aren't what they once were in the Garden State, since it now has some of the strictest environmental controls in the nation. Yet a short bus ride from Hoboken proves that New Jersey still maintains the odd landfill. Today the garbage goes only to feed flocks of sea gulls. In Henderson's day, things were different.

Henderson laid his method out in *Gardening for Profit,* his guide for the would-be market gardener. Take a low-lying part of the garden—an area 50 by 100 feet is ideal—and surround it with a 6-foot-tall fence. Fill the depression with stable or barnyard manure to a depth of 18 or 24 inches. Drive your hogs into the pen— Henderson doesn't say how many, but I figure that a couple of dozen would be sufficient—so that they may stir the muck with their feet. And all that wilted produce you couldn't sell to the New Yorkers? That goes to feed the hogs, who will start the process of digestion and provide a continual flow of organic matter to keep the muck composting. To this you could also add the bargeload of garbage New Yorkers were sending your way; some of the contents were probably the vegetables you had sold.

In this fashion my hero was able to recycle all his rotten cabbages (and who knows what else) and turn them into cash while also saving himself the cost of fertilizer. What's more, his composting method provided bacon for all those breakfasts he had no time to eat. This elegant solution to the problem of solid waste disposal is one that Tom intends to revive—as soon as he can persuade Marty to fence his backyard.

Underground Composting

The heap offers composters a couple of advantages — it helps in keeping the compostables aerated and by improving drainage protects them from drowning. But as Sir Albert Howard proved, it isn't the only way to go. Pit composting, as underground composting is most often called, has a devoted, if smaller, band of practitioners, and does have some special virtues.

The basic procedure for underground composting is the same as for the usual, upwardly mobile kind, except that you begin by excavating a hole. Since the surrounding soil provides excellent insulation, you don't have to worry so much about achieving a critical mass. Try digging out a space a couple of feet across and a foot or more deep, and be sure to choose a well-drained spot for this, such as the side of a hill or on top of a little rise, so that your compost pit doesn't turn into a well with the first rain. Then dump your organic garbage into the hole as it accumulates, covering each new load with a layer of loose soil.

Unlike composting in a heap, where air can work its way in from the sides, much of the decomposition in the pit will be anaerobic. As we noted in Chapter 1 that means the decay will produce rotten-smelling hydrogen sulfide gas — and other odoriferous vapors. But if you keep the compostables covered with soil until the decay is finished, the stink will be contained. Actually, many pit composters *never* remove the compost from the hole. Instead, they locate their pits where they plan to set a tree or shrub, or maybe a vegetable patch. Then, after the decomposition is complete, they set the transplants right into the compost.

There are some regions of the country to which pit composting is peculiarly adapted. In a hot, dry climate, composting in the ground rather than over it will markedly reduce water usage, since moisture won't evaporate off the sides of the heap. This savings can be significant in arid regions where water is expensive and may be crucial to carrying on through droughts when water use is restricted. If we were composting in Phoenix or Los Angeles, we would definitely sink our heaps.

Likewise, in the far north, pit composting may prove more practical than composting in heaps. There, sinking the compostables into the ground provides protection from frost that will dramatically lengthen the composting season. Long after a heap has frozen solid, the pit will keep on perking.

For those who compost out of a sense of duty rather than enthusiasm for the craft, pit composting offers one more advantage. Because the composting waste is probably going to turn anaerobic (slimy and stinky) anyway, you don't have to take as much care with your blend of ingredients. Just make sure to open no pit before its time.

The Case Against Liming

Sir Albert's addition of lime to his heaps and pits may have been based on common sense, but compost scientists have since learned that it takes a hidden toll. The level of hydrogen ions in a material, a measure of its relative acidity or alkalinity, is expressed in a number, the "pH." This may range from 1.0 (extremely acidic; lemon juice has a pH of 2.0) to 14.0 (extremely alkaline; baking soda's pH is only 8.5 or so). A pH of 7.0 is neutral—neither acidic nor alkaline, and that is the pH most decomposers prefer.

According to Dr. Clarence Golueke (formerly a research biologist with the University of California at Berkeley), most bacteria flourish best within a range of 6.0–7.5; fungal decomposers are more tolerant, thriving in a pH anywhere from 5.5 to 8.0.[5] This means that if you stock the heap with acidic materials such as tree leaves, fresh manures, or even vegetable scraps, you may, by dropping the heap's overall pH below the ideal level, retard decomposition somewhat.

A dose of lime is the gardener's stock response to excessive acidity, since it is strongly alkaline and neutralizes acids, quickly adjusting a soil or compost's pH upward. Tossing in a handful of lime per layer as Howard suggested may indeed increase bacterial activity within your heap and so accelerate decomposition. But this greater speed comes at a cost. For as the pH rises, the nitrogen in the heap begins to volatilize and escape as gaseous ammonia. So while you increase the speed of decomposition, you rob its product of much of its value.

A far better way to temper the effect of any acidic substance is to feed your heap a varied diet. That way, you practically ensure that no one material can drastically alter the pH. Golueke's final word on this subject was not to worry. Eventually, the composting bacteria will digest any acids too, so that as the heap matures, the pH will rise toward the neutral zone all by itself.[6]

Indoor Composting

Maybe your landscape doesn't extend beyond a fourteenth-story terrace. There's simply no room for a compost heap there. Yet your plants (and though they are few, they are all the more precious for that reason) need humus as much as any, and you don't like the idea

---

[5] Clarence Golueke, *Composting: A Study of the Process and Its Principles* (Emmaus, PA: Rodale Press, 1972), pp. 30–31.
[6] Golueke, p. 41.

of sending your organic garbage to the landfill. You move the composting indoors.

Our limited experience with indoor composting confirms what its proponents claim: it is acceptably sanitary and odor free, and if handled right it yields remarkably quick results.

Your basic equipment is a squat, open-mouthed container. A plastic bucket with some sort of loose lid would work fine, but we went the thrifty route of adapting an empty gallon milk jug. To ready this for its new role, we decapitated it below the handle, leaving a small tag of plastic intact to serve as a hinge. Our next step was to take a day's-worth of vegetable wastes, coffee grounds, and stale bread and chop them up fine; we found that our long-suffering blender was the best tool for that.

What emerged was something that looked like guacamole gone wrong and that smelled . . . like garbage. We drained off the excess liquid, and spread the gunk in a layer across the bottom of our modified jug. Next, we covered the minicomposter's contents with a layer of soil. We stole ours from a compost-enriched flower bed outside the kitchen door, so we knew it contained all the necessary decomposers, but if you must buy bagged soil, make sure that what you get hasn't been sterilized.

We added another layer of garbage purée every day or two, covering each one with another layer of soil to contain the odor and help absorb the liquid. Waterlogging proved this process's greatest problem, for the vegetable scraps and coffee grounds both brought a lot of moisture with them. Periodically, we drained off any liquid that accumulated in the bottom of the jug, and we stirred the composting garbage every day to aerate it. Even so, the composting that took place was at least partially anaerobic, judging by the sour smell of the jug's contents. The loose cover provided by the jug's top contained most of the odor, however, and an unsympathetic observer (Tom's wife, Suzanne) admitted that you really couldn't smell anything unless you stuck your nose right down by the minicomposter's opening.

As soon as we had filled the container to the two-thirds mark, we set it aside to age—though even after we stopped adding new garbage, we continued to stir the compost daily. If we had wanted to continue the experiment, we could have started another jug, of course. As it was, our indoor composting was completed in about a month; depending on how much organic waste *you* generate, and how many jugs you fill, you could find yourself harvesting a gallon or two of black, crumbly compost every couple of weeks.

Another technique for the indoor composter (one that comes highly recommended by horticulturist and friend Elvin MacDonald) is to collect your wastes until you've got one or two bucketfuls and then dump them into a black plastic bag. Moisten the contents (if that's necessary—once again, don't drown them), seal the bag, and set it in a sunny window. Once a day, remix the contents by rolling the bag around for a minute. The composting in this case will certainly be anaerobic, but since the stench will be contained, that doesn't matter. Be sure to open the bag outdoors, though, when you want to check the composting's progress—this type of composting should complete itself within two or three months.

What to do with the compost you make is, of course, your business. But if your house plants can't absorb the whole crop, may we suggest taking the excess to the park? What you spread around the shrubbery there may be the first fresh humus those plants have tasted since the Indians moved out, and the whites, with their rakes and landfills, moved in.

Sheet Composting

We've saved this composting method for last because Tom doesn't approve—it disproves all his theories about good composting being the product of hard work. Sheet composting works like an extended version of Marty's Uriah Heap. You spread the compostables at the end of the growing season over an area you intend to plant the following year, and then you rototill them into the soil to rot in place. After that, the only effort you need make is to mulch the area with a thick (2- to 6-inch) layer of spoiled hay or straw—by keeping the soil moist and insulating it from the cold weather, you enhance decomposition.

There are a few drawbacks to this method (besides the fact that it strikes Tom as shiftless). Because the organic wastes never heat up, weed seeds and pathogens survive to rear their ugly heads the following spring. Also, if you add too much carbon-rich material to the soil in this fashion, it will deplete its nitrogen reserves as it decays. That problem is only temporary, since when the compostables finally do decay they will gradually release the nitrogen they absorbed along the way. Still, rototill 6 inches of autumn leaves into your vegetable patch (as some so-called experts advise) and, unless you add repeated doses of nitrogen fertilizers, you are looking forward to a sparse and stunted crop for the next year or two.

You can avoid fertility problems by taking care to incorporate plenty of nitrogen-rich material into your sheet composting. By taking care to keep the sheet compost free of weeds and obviously buggy or diseased material, you can limit the problems you pass along to next year's crop, too. Sheet composting does have its liabilities, and it isn't elegant. It's the easiest way to dispose of large quantities of organic debris, though, and a practical way to revive large areas of soil quickly. ·

CHAPTER **7**

High Tech and Hard Sell — A Consumer's Guide to Composting

ONCE UPON A TIME, there was a spiritual purity to the act of composting: it was just you (the local oddball) out back, alone with your heap and nature. Boy, have things changed.

Today the average composter must wait until dark if he would sneak out to the heap without fighting his way through a crowd of salesmen. And his heap isn't a heap anymore—the compostables are all neatly packaged in one of those superefficient and superexpensive designer bins. Chances are, too, that what the composter is stuffing into the bin is mostly catalogues, those catalogues that the composting suppliers send out in the multimillions now.

Composting is big business today. Those same executives who spend their days designing ever more elaborate and bulky packaging for hamburgers have real-

151

ized that by gorging our landfills, they've created an enormous market for recycling devices. So without a trace of shame, U.S. industry has jumped into a phone booth and emerged clad all in green. It's working now to persuade you that decomposers can't function unless they are properly accessorized. Those accessories aren't cheap, either. Outfitting a state-of-the-art compost heap can easily run into thousands of dollars.

One reasonable response to this situation is to refuse to buy anything. We've tried that route, it works, and in the next few pages we'll tell you how. But we're human—we love toys as much as anyone else, and we haven't been able to resist *all* the gadgets the composting industrial complex has produced. We've found that many are kind of fun to use, and that some actually work.[1]

Before sharing those experiences with you, though, we feel obliged to outline the no-cost approach. That was researched in its purest form by Tom's mother.

For years, her only composting tool was a spade. She was a classic pit composter (though we're not sure she'd appreciate this label). Periodically she would find a pri-

---

[1] We considered trying to compile a detailed, comparative chart of composters and accessories, but in the end we decided we wouldn't. In part that was because of the overwhelming number of products on the market; there are hundreds of composters out there, we learned, and innumerable accessories. Testing and comparing all those gadgets would take years of painstaking effort, and neither Tom nor Marty would volunteer for that. Anyway, the gadgetry really doesn't deserve that kind of effort. No matter what wrapper you put the compostables in, the process of decay remains basically the same, and that means the choice of a compost bin (or the choice to avoid one altogether) is mostly idiosyncratic.

So in that spirit we offer a supremely idiosyncratic guide. If you do go shopping for a compost bin, though, we suggest you refer to Joe Keyser's hints for shoppers. In addition, in the Appendix you'll find addresses for more catalogues than you can ever possibly read.

vate spot behind the shrubbery, dig a hole, and start her own minilandfill. But her homemade version *did* promote decay, and every few months she would have another deposit of finished, odor-free compost for her garden. Her technique was simple and effective.

Yet though this system worked well, Tom's mother eventually developed a longing for a bin. Maybe it was the subliminal suggestion of all the pictures she was seeing in her seed and nursery catalogues. Whatever the reason, she had to have one, but she wasn't about to spend money on the thing.

Instead, she picked up four wooden loading pallets that were being thrown away by a local lumberyard. Standing these on their sides, she arranged them in a square and tied them together at the corners with old clothesline. This slapdash structure worked well too; it kept the garbage contained but allowed plenty of air to filter in through the cracks between the boards. To protect the composting materials from rain, she draped a plastic trash bag over the top of the bin, and within months Mother was once again turning out premium compost.

While Tom admired his mother's thrift and ingenuity, he wasn't inclined to follow her example. He admits to being a bit fussy (just a bit) and he'd as soon keep an old washing machine on the front porch as decorate his backyard with loading pallets. He was going to build his own composter too, but what he had in mind was a fancy, three-compartment model with walls of galvanized wire fencing, sliding doors, and a removable cover.

The frame for this was supposed to be made from scrap lumber. But when Tom went down to the lumberyard to get the fencing for the walls (he used a medium-weight grade called "dog wire") he couldn't resist the handsome, pressure-treated 2-by-4's he saw there. Once he had taken that step, he obviously couldn't bang the thing together with nails. Instead, he invested several more dollars in steel corner braces. The front doors he made of pressure-treated 1-by-6's, and with the scrap from them and two panels of corrugated fiberglass paneling he put together a really elegant vaulted roof.

All in all, this project consumed almost $100 in materials and a full weekend of labor. Tom's wife referred to the result as "that Cadillac composter." Did he care? The composter worked like a Cadillac, and all Tom's composting friends were envious.

Meanwhile, Marty was taking the first steps forward from the Uriah Heap. What follows is his report from the frontiers of technologically assisted decomposition:

In the interest of untrammeled scientific investigation, I performed an experiment last fall. After the leaves had fallen, I made a huge pile of leaves, twigs, debris from the garden, and grass clippings that I had been saving from the summer plus assorted kitchen refuse. I divided the debris into three piles. I placed one pile in a composting "barrel." That's a gadget that suspends what looks like an old pickle barrel from some plastic tubes so you can give it a spin and thereby mix the ingredients and add air. I placed the second pile in a green plastic silo with holes in the side for air to enter and a cone-shaped top that allegedly speeds up heating while keeping too much rain from getting in. And I placed the third pile, as I have traditionally done, in a corner of the garden between my last evergreen and my neighbor's used car farm next door. Here's what happened:

October 1. All systems up and running. I'm impressed by how neat the barrel and silo look and what an unsightly mess the stuff outside is. Unfortunately, when I turn the barrel I realize that I have neglected to fasten the top tightly and I find myself knee-deep in wet leaves and old grapefruits. Fortunately my children are not within hearing distance when I react.

November 1. The outside pile looks exactly the same. Something is definitely happening in the silo, since it feels quite warm to the touch when I remove the top to stir the contents around a bit with a pitchfork. But when I do this, I see that I have not fastened the sides of the plastic sheet together exactly right and the silo starts to collapse. I put my arms around it as if we are about to make love and scream for my son to come put the plastic tab back in the slot so the whole thing doesn't collapse. "How much is it worth to you?" he asks.

December 1. It's still pretty warm for this time of year, daytime temperatures around 50°F, nighttime around freezing. The outdoor pile seems to be shrinking and I notice that a few of the neighborhood dogs have decided to make a contribution to the effort.

January 1. If you think I'm going to go outside to check compost on New Year's Day, you have no idea how much they pay you for writing a book like this.

February 1. The outside pile is covered with snow. I approach the barrel tentatively. Making sure the top is secure, I give it a spin. The plastic tubing holding it promptly collapses and the barrel lands on my foot. I'd say the thing weighs at least 50 to 75 pounds. When I go into work limping the next morning, I say it's the result of a football injury.

March 1. The calendar may say spring is on the way, but we had our biggest snow of the year yesterday, about 8 inches or so. I can barely make out the pile in the back so I have no idea what's going on there. The only way I can tell where it is amid the white is by the markers the local dogs have thoughtfully placed there for me. There's no way I'm going near the barrel with all this ice and snow on the ground. As a matter of fact, I think I'll skip the silo as well and go in, have a drink, and wait for spring.

April 1. And by god, here it is, spring at last. Last night we had over a foot of snow. Back into the house to look at seed catalogues.

May 1. The backyard pile is definitely cooking. I can tell because Kiki, our Siamese cat, has been sitting on it, valiantly fending off the dogs and getting her daily sauna. The pile is approximately half its original size. Since the tubing for the barrel has more or less disintegrated, I now simply roll it around on the ground. In spite of my problems with it, the dang-blasted thing seems to be working. It looks to me like everything in it is pretty well cooked. As for the silo, I can't see a heck of a lot of difference between its contents and the pile outside.

June 1. I've applied the stuff in the barrel to the garden. There are still some undigested grapefruits plus a volleyball (?!!!) in the silo, so I think I'll wait another month with that. The outside pile seems pretty well cooked. The main problem with it is that it's about a hundred feet from the garden. I call my son and offer him five bucks if he'll load it onto the wheelbarrow and bring it over. He suddenly remembers an important exam he has the next day. I decide to spread the compost around the evergreens to see if I can hide a bit of the view of the neighbor's decaying cars.

July 1. The tomatoes are tomatoeing. We've already had a great crop of beans. The roses are red, violets are blue. . . . The evergreens are great, but the guy's now moved a decaying pickup truck in as well. Oh well, I suppose it will compost eventually.

August 1. As my crops mature, I use the barrel to store stalks, stems, leaves, etc., which I will mix with the leaves when they start to fall next month.

What are my conclusions from this venture into high-tech composting?

1. Sooner or later, compost happens.

2. Barrels are sort of convenient, but scratch the housing and just roll them around.

3. The silo hides the compost, but aside from that I really couldn't see much of a difference.

4. If you can figure out a way to get a teenager to work, write me care of the publisher. Thanks.

Marty's adventures left Tom dissatisfied. Tom insisted that his homemade composter had a sincerity that Marty's recycled pickle barrel lacked. Still, he couldn't help admiring the panache of the off-the-shelf models. Fortunately, the research for this book clearly demanded that Tom also acquire and test as many composters as possible. As it happened, he already had one picked out: Rubbermaid's new 18-cubic-foot-capacity, double-walled composter.

"Stop Throwing the Earth Away" urged the advertisement. This unit was going to help Tom discover the valuable resources in his own yard, and unlike his homemade composter, its plastic walls were insulated so that he would be able to compost year-round. Louvers around the composter's base would ensure proper aeration. Not only that, but it carried a six-year guarantee.

The composter arrived around the middle of February, and it took maybe three minutes to assemble; the only tool required was a fist, which Tom used to bang the interlocking tabs into position. It was, as promised, an "attractive green," and really, it looked more like a dog house than a composter. Tom's only complaint, initially, was that someone had stolen the concept for this book. "Compost this box!" seemed to be Rubbermaid's new motto, for it had been printed with nontoxic, water-soluble ink and the composter's instructions advised that the customer should make it the first entry to the bin.

Referring to his composting journal, Tom finds that besides the well-soaked fragments of cardboard (the Rubbermaid instructions advised wetting the box thoroughly and tearing it into 1-inch-wide pieces), he filled the bin with a mixture of shredded leaves and fresh (steaming!) horse manure. That was on February 15, when it was cold enough that Tom could wet the compostables with snow instead of water. By the next morning, probing with a thermometer revealed that the temperature at the compostables' center was 64°F, well above the ambient temperature of 50°F.

By that afternoon the compostables had reached a temperature of 77°F, and on the 20th (five days after loading) the temperature inside the bin stood at 110°F. Meanwhile, the materials in Tom's wire and wood, homemade composter remained at more or less the same temperature as the surrounding air.

Three days later (February 23) the temperature in the Rubbermaid composter peaked at 140°F. White threads of mold had covered everything inside, the compostables were steaming, and water was condensing on the composter's pitched plastic roof. Already the contents had subsided 4–5 inches. The next day, the temperature of the compostables started to drop. Even though Tom aerated the materials inside the bin by turning them with a fork, and began adding vegetable scraps to supply more nitrogen, the bin continued to cool, dropping to back to ambient by the end of the month. On the 5th of March, the end of a brief cold snap let the air temperature creep back up to 48°F; inside the bin, it stayed at 41°F.

Tom rates the Rubbermaid bin only a partial success, and he thinks a clue lies in its water consumption. Other composters he has used need watering every few weeks, especially if the compost inside is hot. Water vapor is one of the by-products of decomposition, and it escapes from the bin into the surrounding atmosphere. The Rubbermaid bin showed little or no need for watering, and Tom suspects that was because there was very little passage of air in or out. That would help create an anaerobic condition in the compostables and account for the sudden drop in temperature after the first couple of weeks.

Whatever the real reason, however, what happened was that after the fast, strong start, composting proceeded so slowly in the Rubbermaid bin that it wasn't until well into summer that the process was complete. Maybe Tom could have accelerated the decay by leaving the top off the bin or by turning the contents more often (though he did toss them several times). In the event, though, his homemade bin processed a similar load of materials much more quickly, even though they remained frozen for the first several weeks.

About the same time as Tom was installing the insulated bin, he saw a note in a gardening newsletter about something even more exciting: solar-powered composting! The means for this was the "Green Cone," a Canadian device that not only promised to harvest heat from the sun and keep the garbage perking right through the coldest winter (down to $-30°F$ was the promise) but also to process things Tom couldn't put in the other bins: meat and fish scraps, oils, fat, even bones. Besides, it was manufactured from 60 percent recycled materials.

How could he say no? Unfortunately, though, by the time the Green Cone arrived, Tom had run out of garbage. What with the demands of his homemade bin, the Rubbermaid bin, and his worms (we'll get to them in a couple of pages), his organic wastes were all bespoken. Tom briefly considered asking the neighbors if he could have their garbage, but decided they might think that strange. Instead, he contacted a sympathetic sort up the street who after a long silence agreed that yes, she supposed he could install the contraption in her yard.

The Cone required a bit more assembly than the Rubbermaid bin—it involved a few screws, but still, it didn't tax even Tom's modest mechanical abilities. An outer translucent cone of green plastic fit over an opaque liner to create a solar heat trap; and the pair of them sat atop a perforated plastic container that was supposed to be set into the ground. Compostables were fed in through a hatch in the top, which was crossed by a safety bar that would, presumably, prevent a child from self-composting. The hinged cover latched securely so that the whole would not become a feeding station for raccoons.

How's it going, Tom would periodically ask his neighbor. "OK" was the only response he would get — apparently, his neighbor wasn't particularly interested in what was going on inside the Cone, as long as there were no repercussions outside. So Tom kept himself busy by polishing up his linguistic skills with the Green Cone manual—the *Manuel d'Instructions,* that, being Canadian, was printed in parallel texts of French and English.

There he read of *"la soupe toxique que l'on appelle 'leachate'"*—the toxic soup or leachate that might contaminate our groundwater if garbage were sent to the landfill instead of the Cone. Tom shuddered at the account of *"le methane"* that infiltrates the earth around the landfills, causing *"des explosions."* He, like the anonymous author, dreamed of dumps free of *"rongeurs"* and *"mouettes"* (rodents and gulls sound much more sophisticated in French).

At the end of the summer, Tom's composting surrogate moved to a new house, and Tom reclaimed his Cone. Having by now liberated his worms and given the Rubbermaid bin to his mother (who immediately abandoned the pallets), Tom had an abundance of garbage once again and was able to solar compost in his own front yard. In digging up the Cone's base, he found in it nothing useful to plants. The basket was empty except for a deposit of unsavory gray goo, and this has since persuaded him that the Cone is more accurately described as a digester than a composter.

But as his friend kept telling him, it works. Dump

any kind of organic garbage into the hatch and forget all about it has been Tom's experience. The Cone came with a box of some mysterious "accelerator," an "organic" powder that supposedly if sifted over the contents of the basket enhances decomposition and controls odor, but Tom has not found its use necessary yet. Naturally Tom is reluctant to devote organic waste to anything that doesn't produce humus, but most of what he puts in the Cone—meat scraps, bones, etc.—would otherwise go into the garbage can, so the loss is slight. Most of the vegetable peels, coffee grounds—all the good stuff—go into the Cadillac out back.

The Cone is effective as a solar energy collector. On a series of recent January afternoons, Tom found the temperature inside the Cone to be as much as 50°F, while outside the puddles of water remained frozen solid. That means that digestion is proceeding, at least slowly. He suspects that next summer, the Cone will literally cook. In the meantime, he's found a benefit never mentioned in advertisements for the Cone, not even in that cosmopolitan manual. The Cone is indeed proving secure against scavengers, and its consumption of all the household's meat and dairy wastes means that *"les ratons laveurs"* (can you imagine calling a raccoon a "washing rat"?) no longer bother to dump Tom's garbage cans.

So Call Me Freudian . . .

We first heard of worm composting two years ago, and the news filled us with a special dread. The reason? The article in the gardening magazine came from California, and we know that if the Californians are doing it, no matter how knuckleheaded the activity may be, a year or two later *everyone* on the East Coast will feel obliged to follow suit. *WE* are the ones who end up drinking blush zinfandel and wine coolers long after the Californians have abandoned that swill. That's why we've started ranching llamas in rural New England, though nobody there has a clue what to do with them. Like it or not, we knew that everyone was going to have a barrel full of garbage-eating worms in their kitchen before long.

What was worse, we knew that this book made it necessary for one of us to try worm composting. After some discussion (*Marty:* No way! *Tom:* Oh, come on. *Marty:* Absolutely not!), it was decided that Tom was the best person for this job. He read up on the habits of earthworms, then he called Carter's Worm Farm in Plains, Georgia, to place an order.

The address rang a bell, and sure enough, it turned out that the proprietor, Hugh Carter, is a first cousin of Mister Jimmy. That, of course, makes perfect sense. Wormpits and snakepits bear a close resemblance, and the same family values that enabled a basically decent man like James Earl Carter to survive four years in Washington have no doubt served his cousin well in the worm business. Or "the worm bid-ness," as they say in Plains.

At any rate, Hugh recommended that Tom start with red wigglers. The advantage of the red wigglers, Hugh explained, is that they stay put. Ordinary earthworms like to roam, but a red wiggler, wherever he/she (these worms are hermaphroditic) finds food, moisture, and appropriate bedding, that's where it stays. Tom ordered 2,000 of Hugh's "Hybrid Breeders," since the Californian articles specified that number as sufficient to stock one "vermi-bin."

While waiting for the livestock to arrive, Tom prepared its home. The articles included elaborate exploded plans of build-it-yourself wooden worm chests, but Tom opted to adapt a plastic garbage barrel. He installed plastic louvered vents around the bottom, the same kind you use to ventilate under the eaves, since the articles all agreed that worms couldn't abide soggy conditions. Then Tom filled the can with brown wrapping paper torn into strips, and moistened them with 3 gallons of hot water. Finally he dumped in half a 2-gallon bucketful of garden soil to provide the grit with which worms fill their gizzards and grind their food. About this time, the worms arrived.

Tom, of course, had bought worms before, in preparation for fishing expeditions, and a dozen (along with their moss bedding) had filled a pint-sized cardboard container. This time Tom was expecting an *enormous* cardboard tub. What he got, though, was a little box about 6 inches to a side. When he ripped this open, he found that it was solid worms inside—the cube of red, slimy meat kept its shape perfectly for a minute or two after Tom dumped it onto the counter, then wiggling arms began to pull themselves free, just like something in a horror movie. Tom quickly pushed the writhing mess into the barrel, snapped on the lid, and toted the whole thing down to the basement.

Early the next morning, Tom's two-year-old son, Matthew, and Matthew's mother, Suzanne, went to greet the new arrivals. They found that these red worms had not read the articles; the worms were *not* staying put, they were in the midst of a great escape, wriggling off in every direction in search of . . . who knew what? For months afterward, though, any time Tom opened a box that had been stored in the basement, he was sure to find a few mummified Georgian worms.

Matthew had watched as his mother gathered up all the worms she could find, and he was all right until she lifted the barrel's lid. Gooey, red blobs dripped off it— the worms had climbed up onto the ceiling of their new home. Matthew shrieked; Tom was impressed when he heard about this, because he hadn't believed it was possible to gross out a two-year-old.

In a day or two, the worms settled down. Tom started them off on a diet of coffee grounds, as the articles suggested. But by the end of the third week he was adding increasing quantities of organic garbage—he would dig a hole in the bedding, drop in the garbage, and pull the shredded paper over it. At the end of their first month in residence the worms were consuming all that Tom, Matthew, and Suzanne could produce.

With the onset of summer, Tom was able to move the worms out of the basement and into the garage. There was still the odd escape, but as the more adventurous part of the population selected itself out, the worms as a group showed less tendency to wander. Liquid from the garbage accumulated in the bottom of the barrel, threatening to turn the worm bedding toxic, so Tom punched holes in the barrel's bottom. Then the evil fluid ran out over the floor until Tom moved the worm composter onto an absorbent pad of old newspaper. The smell inside the barrel was sour, but not intolerable, and it didn't spread to fill the garage. Every couple of months, Tom would top up the barrel with a fresh supply of paper as the old bedding disintegrated.

While poking garbage down into the mass of worms, sodden paper, and last week's assorted refuse was never as much fun as the articles had promised, still, it wasn't too bad. Tom didn't dislike worms per se—he had baited his own hook from an early age and felt a certain amount of gratitude toward the creatures that had provided so much sport. But his enthusiasm for fishing was precisely why he found his red wigglers so disappointing.

When he ordered the worms, he had also invested in a full set of the booklets Hugh Carter had written about the big money in worms (*18 Secrets of Successful*

Worm Raising, Over 300 Questions and Answers on Worm Raising, How and Where to Sell Fishworms and Crickets, etc.). This literature had filled Tom with dreams of a worm empire. If his worms doubled in population every two months (as they were supposed to), in a year he'd be harvesting a thousand a day. Surely he could sell them for a penny apiece—maybe 2 or 3 cents each—and that meant he could retire the word processor.

Reality intruded. Tom's worms seemed to multiply just fine (although he never actually counted them) but they never increased in size from the scrawny inchworm size they'd been on arrival. Maybe you could thread one of them onto a trout hook, but Tom doubted there was much of a market. By fall he had concluded that while these hybrid breeders might consume garbage they were never going to earn their keep any other way. One warm, Indian summer day Tom liberated the worms into the garden. Let them dig their way back to Georgia.

Worms weren't the only thing that came out of the barrel when Tom tipped it over; a couple of bucketfuls of black muck slid out too. So the worms *did* produce a usable compost. So what. Tom could have processed the garbage much more easily in his bin, and escaped all those close encounters of the slimy kind.[2]

Don't be uptight, the articles had urged. Worms are

---

[2]Those who want to harvest the compost without losing their worms should tip the whole mess—worms, bedding, and so on—from one barrel into another. That will reverse the stratigraphy, leaving the finished compost on top and the fresh bedding on the bottom. Then set the barrel out in a sunny spot for a half hour or so, so that the heat and light drive the worms down into the barrel's depths. The black, finished compost may then be scooped out, after which the remaining worms and bedding can be tipped back into the original bin and returned to the garage.

natural, and natural is beautiful, right? There must be something *wrong* with you if you don't want to keep a barrel full of worms in your kitchen. Probably it's a sexual problem.

Probably. But Tom has no problem with his sense of irony, and he takes great pleasure in hearing from gardening friends here in the East about how *wonderful* their worms are, how they really *like* catering to invertebrates. Because Tom is sure that by now the Californian worm bins are derelict, gathering dust alongside those half-empty bottles of blush Zinfandel. The trend-setters out there are already up to something new, he's sure.

The Greatest in the Galaxy—

We are sure that some things about our nation's capital would disturb George Washington ("Father, I cannot tell a lie; Saddam Hussein cut down your cherry tree"). But as noted in Chapter 2, the father of our country was a composter, and so we are confident that he would thoroughly approve of the National Home Composting Park.

Actually, it's set on one of George's properties—not Mount Vernon, but the River Farm that the president maintained nearby. The park occupies only a tiny fraction of the property, which is now the home of the American Horticultural Society. In all, composters cover an area of *maybe* 60 by 80 feet. Nevertheless, this is the largest collection of composting units in the country. Indeed, as curator Joe Keyser pointed out, it's probably the largest collection in the galaxy.

Joe is not a horticulturist by training, nor even a sanitation engineer. He's a medievalist, with a master's degree from Georgetown University. Maybe it's the trace of Brooklyn in his voice that explains why Joe is so comfortable among the odd and futuristic hardware—he claims that Brooklynites dominate the home composting field. Whatever the truth of that, Joe had eighty-five composters up and running on the day we visited, though he was quick to assure us that his whole collection ran to more than ninety-five; the others he has put to work at churches, nature centers, and various other sites around the metropolitan Washington area.

How does a medievalist end up with a corner on composters? More or less by accident. As a dedicated home gardener and keen outdoorsman, he had moved into environmental journalism after completing his degree, and had eventually come to the Horticultural Society to work in program development and marketing. He had wanted to install a composter in the gardens there—he couldn't imagine a garden without one. It seemed reasonable to share this experience with the public too, and Joe planned an informal workshop. He was surprised when, in response to his press release, the Washington Post sent a reporter and photographer to River Farm; what astonished him, though, was the public response to the newspaper article. Joe, who had anticipated a handful of participants, found himself fielding more than 900 telephone calls.

Soon he was teaching two composting classes a day, and over the next year (1991) he gave 180-odd presentations to a total of 5,400 people. When he sent news of this campaign to the compost manufacturers, donations of equipment began pouring in. And so the "Park" was born.

We arrived for our tour in early February, when all Joe's plantings of heirloom vegetables were dormant. Still, there were clues as to the fertility of the product. What we thought was the frame of a teepee, a cluster of 15-foot-tall bamboo poles, proved to be the trellis onto which Joe trains his lima beans, and he explained to us

FIGURE 10a. Build yourself a bin on the cheap.

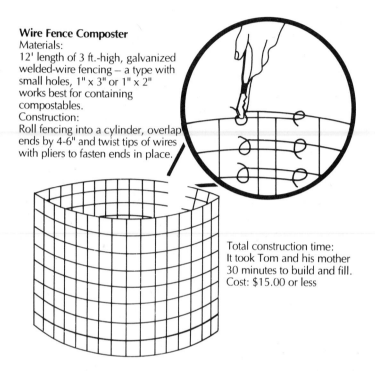

Wire Fence Composter
Materials:
12' length of 3 ft.-high, galvanized welded-wire fencing — a type with small holes, 1" x 3" or 1" x 2" works best for containing compostables.
Construction:
Roll fencing into a cylinder, overlap ends by 4-6" and twist tips of wires with pliers to fasten ends in place.

Total construction time:
It took Tom and his mother 30 minutes to build and fill.
Cost: $15.00 or less

how, come summer, the tomato vines would entirely hide many of the bins. Nor was this phenomenal growth due to the natural fertility of the soil.

To create the site, Joe had filled a gully with sixty truckloads of sticky, impenetrable marine clay, and to this he has added not a single synthetic "conditioner" or fertilizer. With layers of wood chips and the output of his bins, however, he had turned the soil into something so rich, crumbly, and dark that we kept wondering if there was some way we could slip it into the trunk of our car and take it home.

If late winter wasn't the best season to admire the lushness of Joe's plantings, still it did present the com-

FIGURE 10b. And even cheaper . . .

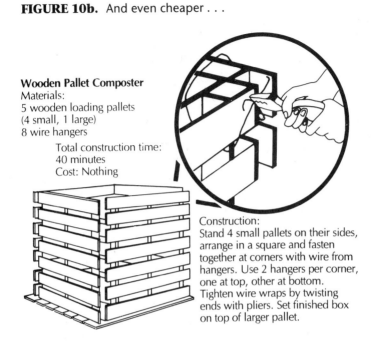

Wooden Pallet Composter
Materials:
5 wooden loading pallets
(4 small, 1 large)
8 wire hangers

Total construction time:
40 minutes
Cost: Nothing

Construction:
Stand 4 small pallets on their sides,
arrange in a square and fasten
together at corners with wire from
hangers. Use 2 hangers per corner,
one at top, other at bottom.
Tighten wire wraps by twisting
ends with pliers. Set finished box
on top of larger pallet.

posters in high relief. There they were: the cones, the crates, the squat silos and boxes of plastic, the little log cabins of cedar wood, the barrels set on tumblers and the rolls and cubes of wire fencing. Which ones were Joe's favorites? The composters he had made himself had a special place in his heart, he confessed.

He especially favored the composters he had fashioned out of wooden pallets, because these addressed two environmental problems. This type of bin is very efficient in degrading wastes, especially if you lay a fifth pallet down inside it as a floor, so that excess water can drain out of the compostables and air can circulate in. Anyway, just in building the bin, a gardener has helped reduce a most serious source of solid waste. Pallet making is the major consumer of hardwoods in the United States; we manufacture a staggering 540 million pallets every year, and fully half of these go to the landfill after a single use. Divert the pallets to the compost heap, and you are doing the environment a double favor.

If you wire the pallets together with old coat hangers as Joe does, then a pallet bin will cost you not a penny. If you want to spend some money, about $2.50, however, Joe notes that you can wrap a fine bin out of a 12½-foot-long piece of galvanized wire fencing. He prefers the type that is 3 feet tall, and whose holes measure about 1 by 3 inches; that's made of a heavy-gauge wire that will stand up in a neat cylinder even when loaded with leaves, scraps, and trash. Once he's loaded a wire bin, Joe likes to surround it with tomatoes. Watering the plants keeps the compostables properly moist, and the nutrients they release as they decompose spur the tomatoes to phenomenal growth.

Joe likes many of the commercial bins as well, and here again he uses price as a fundamental criterion. The perforated sheets of recycled plastic that Willmarc, Inc., sells for $10 apiece are easy to assemble — roll the sheet into a cylinder and snap it together — and unlike competing brands, they are slick on the inside so that when composting is complete you can slip the bin up and off. Another advantage of such plastic sleeves is that they are easy to move or ship since they weigh only 6 pounds each, whereas a wooden bin might weigh 40. Joe also approves of a more elaborate Toro bin that features a lid designed to capture rainwater and feed it into the compostables. A failure to keep the compostables sufficiently moist is the major cause of home composting failures he has found and the benefits of rainwater more than compensate for any loss of nutrients in his opinion.

Moving into the realm of high tech, Joe showed me what looked like a dumpster set on a spit — solar panels attached to the frame power a motor that will automat-

FIGURE 10c. Tom's Cadillac, three-bin composter. Not cheap, but few status symbols are.

3-Bin, Cadillac Composter

All wood should be pressure treated with a wood preservative rated for ground contact.

Materials:

2" x 4" lumber; (3) 9-ft lengths for top and bottom cross-braces, (8) 32" lengths for uprights of bin divides and sides, (8) 36" lengths lengths for tops and bottoms of bin dividers and sides.

1" x 6" decking boards; (18) 34 1/2" lengths to slide into guides on bin fronts.

1" x 4" lumber; (4) 36" lengths, (1) 36" length ripped into 1" x 1" - assemble into guides for front doors.

36" high roll (25 ft. long) of 2 x 3 galvanized welded wire fencing (I used the inexpensive "utility" grade).

Galvanized staples to fasten fencing to wooden frame.

4" corner braces (16) to assemble bin dividers and sides.

5/8" galvanized carriage bolts (12), 4" long, nuts & washers to fasten cross braces to bin dividers and sides.

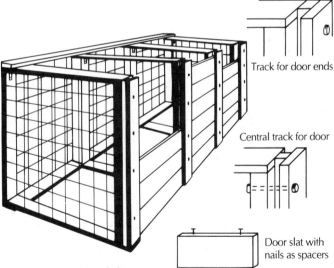

Track for door ends

Central track for door

Door slat with nails as spacers

1/4" galvanized carriage bolts
(16) 4" long, nuts & washers to fasten door frames to front of bin dividers.

Galvanized roofing nails (30) - driven into tops of door slots as spacers to improve aeration of bins.

Construction: See plan
Total construction time: One weekend
Cost: $100.00 - but you'll be the envy of all your fellow composters.

ically turn this giant metal compost box at any interval you select. Sold by Swisher Mower and Machine Co. of Warrensburg, Missouri, for a tidy $500, this unit manufactures compost more efficiently than most of the other rotating drum types because of its square shape. Whereas compostables may slide around in a block inside a turning barrel, in the rectilinear Swisher automaton they tumble from corner to corner. Sure it's expensive, but look at the features—the Swisher machine even includes a hasp so you can padlock the drum shut and protect your compost against theft.

What about the compostable composters made of cardboard? Joe showed me such a thing but dismissed it with a snort—$6 for a bin that may degrade before its contents. He does like the "Tumblebug," though, a twenty-sided plastic polyhedron you roll about the garden to mix its contents. This device processes materials adequately and although it costs $169, it is unique in that it allows you to take the bin to the source of compostables, and later roll the finished product through the garden to dump compost right onto its final resting place.

"Look at the price" is Joe's first tip to anyone shopping for a compost bin. This is especially important since if you are like him you will need not one but two units. Joe defines himself as a "passive" composter, meaning that he doesn't bother with carbon–nitrogen ratios and a hot pile. He dumps whatever he's got into a bin and then, aside from an occasional aeration of the contents, he lets nature take its course. He maintains that this is how most people tackle composting, and it means that the process may take up to a year to complete. So he likes to fill one bin over the course of a year and then let it sit for a year while he fills a second one; by the time the second bin is full, the first bin is ready to empty.

Joe also warns that a bin must allow the composter

easy access. He showed me one or two models that looked like piggy banks, so small and narrow was the loading port—and how, he wanted to know, are you going to get a tool inside to aerate the contents or even remove the finished compost? Look for durable materials—the styrofoam bin he showed me was light and it did help insulate the compostables for better heat conservation and more thermophilic composting, but a careless poke with a fork or shovel would go right through it.

Match the size of your bin to the property; the cultivator of a townhouse garden will never fill a 64-cubic-foot-capacity bin such as the ones Joe makes out of his loading pallets. Similarly, the keeper of a one-acre landscaper will fill one of those cute little 10-cubic-foot plastic boxes in no time. That's one reason why Joe has refused to recommend specific models. Everyone's situation is different, and the best composter for you will depend not only on the size of your yard but also on the amount of garbage you generate and on your personality.

When you do find a composter you like, Joe advises you to shop around—the bin you covet may be available from a number of different distributors and at a dramatic disparity in price. If you can get down to River Farm in Alexandria, Virginia, by all means visit the American Horticultural Society's display (the Composting Park is open from 8:30–5:30, Monday through Friday). If you can't do this, then Joe Keyser recommends sending away for as many catalogues as you can stand (you'll find addresses listed in the Appendix of this book) as well as stopping by the local garden center.

Tom would like to add one last note. His father, who was the WASP toward whom those lightbulb jokes are directed, was a fine gardener but a hopelessly inept mechanic. Having purchased a fancy, multipaneled European drum composter, he spent most of a Saturday inserting plastic tabs into plastic slots and turning plastic screws to assemble the thing. That night he heard a noise and went out into the backyard, flashlight in hand. He arrived just in time to watch a garbage-seeking raccoon finish a tidy disassembly of the new composter.

After several more afternoons of reassembly, and evenings spent stopwatch and flashlight in hand, he came to the humiliating conclusion that the coon was twenty times quicker than he was. We're not sure exactly what conclusions to draw from this, except that it doesn't pay to get too cute. Keep your composting simple. Otherwise you may, like Tom's father, end up sending $200 worth of imported technology straight to the dump.

Activators

Another type of product that features prominently in composting catalogues these days are the "activators," or "starters." These claim to increase biological activity in your bin or heap by supercharging it with the best kinds of microorganisms. Do they work? Yes — but they still aren't worth the money.

The activators produced by reputable manufacturers do offer concentrated doses of bacterial and fungal decomposers. What the merchandisers don't bother to tell you, though, is that similar microorganisms are already present in most garden soils. That's why Tom used to toss a shovelful of earth into his bin from time to time as he was filling it. But he has since learned even that is unnecessary. The fact is that practically any material you would add to your heap — leaves, grass clippings, vegetable parings — are already spotted with decomposers that are waiting and ready to go to work. Organic matter (unless it has been irradiated or something bizarre like that) carries the seeds of its own destruction.

An activator might be useful if your bin sits far from any wild areas and you are trying to endow the compost with fungal antagonists. Even then, however, you are probably better off with a cup or two of real woodland soil than with some mail-order wonder cure.

As for Coca-Cola—and some people seriously recommend dousing the heap with this—we don't have any data about its efficacy as a bioactivator. Since its formula is a well-kept secret, we're not sure if it will compost at all. Certainly, though, using it for this purpose would be better for your teeth.

If You Buy Nothing Else . . .

. . . Get a manure fork. It's the tool that you'll use to heave materials such as straw or manure into the bin or heap, the tool you'll use to mix the materials and later toss and aerate them. It's also the most convenient tool for lifting the finished compost into a wheelbarrow or trash can.

A spading fork, one of those four-pronged jobs with short, square tines you'll find down at the hardware store, is not an adequate substitute. What you want is a *manure* fork, a fork with four long, curving tines that are round in cross-section. The spading fork is designed for turning soil; the manure fork is designed to scoop up and move organic materials, and it does this beautifully.

You'll find manure forks at the local feed store, or failing that you can order them from A. M. Leonard, Inc., 6665 Spiker Rd., P.O. Box 816, Piqua, OH 45356. This tool will cost you somewhere between $30 and $40, and if you don't abuse it or leave it outside to rust, it will last forever.

Thermometers

Aside from a manure fork, these are the serious composter's most essential tool. Marty makes do with his cat, but Tom maintains you cannot compost efficiently without a thermometer to monitor the progress of decay within the heap. He uses a foot-long glass thermometer "borrowed" from his wife the college professor's laboratory—this is superaccurate, and since it is calibrated to the Celsius scale, it keeps Tom's mathematical skills limbered up (to convert a temperature in Celsius to Fahrenheit, multiply the Celsius degrees by $\frac{9}{5}$ and add 32).

If Tom weren't so smart, he would have to order a real composting thermometer, one that's calibrated in degrees Fahrenheit. Available from most garden tool suppliers, such thermometers come equipped with an easy-to-read dial and a sturdy, 20-inch-long, metal-encased probe, and they cost only $18 or so.

Those who refuse to spend any money and whose spouses won't let them into their place of work can make do with a 3-foot length of steel or iron rod. Push it into the center of the heap, leave it there for 10 minutes, then withdraw it and feel the tip. This provides only the roughest guesstimate of the heap's interior temperature, but then someone as cheap as you must be accustomed to inconvenience.

Shredders and Chippers

These machines do accelerate the composting process. By ripping the compostables into bits a shredder greatly increases the surface area exposed to the decomposer and ruptures any protective skin in which nature may have wrapped the organic material. Tom liked his inexpensive leaf shredder so much that he had intended to include a survey of the more heavy-duty types, shredders and chippers that could handle even woody materials.

Then we checked the prices. There are electric models that sell for as little as $250, but they not only look like toys, they perform like them. If you intend to process any volume of material, you'll need one of the gasoline-driven, hammermill machines that *start* at around $800. These are not tools for the enthusiasts, we decided; these are strictly for the fanatics, and the fanatics' number is too few to influence sales of this book. So we canceled the survey.

Tom has found that an old gasoline-powered lawnmower, a rotary model with three or four horsepower, makes an acceptable substitute. It won't handle truly woody materials such as tree or hedge trimmings, but it will shred cornstalks, weeds, or anything of that caliber. Spread the compostables in a layer an inch or two deep, and run the mower back and forth over them.

Joe Keyser insisted that the dust produced by this operation would foul the mower's engine. He suggests that instead you rent a chipper, selecting the biggest, most powerful one you can find. The daily rental fee may seem like a lot of money, but only, Joe says, until you consider what you are getting for the money. He quoted a survey which had found that homeowners who buy chippers use them on average only 11 hours (one long day) every year. For one day's rental, you get the same mechanical assistance as your neighbor who spent maybe $1,000 on a similar machine—and you don't have to worry about maintenance.

Aerators

Maybe you too have been curious about those gizmos that look like the handle of a lawnmower with little flanges mounted on the tip. They are pictured in every composting catalogue these days, and at $14 or so they seem like a steal. Simply plunge the aerator into your heap and yank it out—do this a dozen times, and *voilà!* The heap is aerated.

Joe Keyser says this really works, and who are we to argue? Still, Tom maintains that he does a much more thorough job of aerating the heap by tossing it like a salad with his manure fork. Joe calls compost aerators a necessity; Tom insists that they rank with snake oil and electric toothbrushes in terms of genuine utility. It's your call.

CHAPTER 8

Look, Ma, It's Compost— Now What Do I Do with It?

I<small>F YOU'VE BEEN</small> following our advice, by now the compost is accumulating in dark brown piles across the back of your yard. (Actually, if you've tried *everything* we've suggested, those piles may be threatening to bury your yard and house, too.) You've got compost, plenty of it; now what are you going to do with it?

As usual, we've got some suggestions. Tom will tell you how to use every bit of what you can degrade in your garden—and if you don't have a garden and don't want one, you can skip ahead to Marty's tips.

But first:

1. The Lawn

We're beginning with this because it is the one application for compost both Tom and Marty endorse. Like most homeowners, they both have lawns, and they've found that the grass needs most of what they can produce.

Lawns have become a popular target of environmentally conscious gardeners in recent years, and with some reason. As currently managed, turf absorbs an astonishing quantity of resources in most U.S. communities. As a nation, we apply more nitrogen fertilizers to our lawns each year than the total consumed by all the farmers of the Indian subcontinent. In many U.S. towns, half of all the water taken from the public supply in summertime is used to irrigate lawns — and this problem is worst in precisely those desert areas where water is in the shortest supply. Finally, the turf maintenance industry is a major vehicle for introducing chemical poisons into the environment.

Just to cure our grass of diseases such as "brown patch" or "dollar spot," we Americans douse it with $55 million worth of fungicides every year. That's 13 percent of all the money we spend on fungicides for every purpose. What makes this even worse is that the lawn care chemicals tend to be "broad spectrum"—that is, they are designed to have a wide-ranging toxicity. In addition, turf fungicides are for the most part long-lived once released into the environment.

Fungicides are only part of the toxic brew, too. Insecticides and weed killers are also included in the sprays and dusts that are applied to 25 million acres of American turf every year. How harmful these materials are is anybody's guess, too, since thirty-four of the thirty-five chemicals most commonly used for this purpose have never been fully evaluated for their safety by the Environmental Protection Agency.

Obviously the lawn chemicals are bad for the wildlife, but this is one kind of pollution that may be even worse for you. After all, you live right in the middle of the target. The danger is worst for the well-to-do: in wealthy neighborhoods, the spray trucks may service up to 90 percent of the lawns. But everybody except the residents of inner cities is at risk. A study conducted in 1987 found that in a typical American suburb, 8,000 homeowners were exposed to lawn pesticides every year.[1]

We'd like to expose them to compost instead. Believe it or not, that's the answer to every one of the lawn's environmental faults. Compost can supply all the nutrients that healthy grass needs; by increasing the water-holding capacity of the soil, it helps a lawn absorb more of the natural precipitation; and as we learned in Chapter 4, compost can substitute for chemical fungicides.

Besides, applying compost to your lawn is a tradition. Fifty years ago, that's what every good greenskeeper did. Look at the old guides to lawn maintenance and you'll find them full of calls for "top-dressings," and what that refers to is the thin coats of decayed organic matters—most often leafmold or well-rotted manures—that gardeners would sprinkle over the turf every fall. That's what we recommend you do with your compost, too. Our only point of disagreement with this classic prescription is that we suggest you give the lawn a dose in springtime, too.

It's a simple process. First, if your lawn is thin or mossy, we recommend that you work it over with an aerator, one of those machines that punches little cores out of the soil. Aerators are available at most tool rental shops, and their effect is to increase the ability of air and

---

[1]These figures I have taken from Eric Nelson's published work, *Biological Control of Turfgrass Diseases,* Cornell Cooperative Extension Information Bulletin 220, Cornell University, Ithaca, NY.

water to penetrate down to the grass roots. They also speed the top-dressing's transformation of the soil, since as the compost settles into the holes left by the cores, it immediately mixes with the top layer of soil. If your lawn appears reasonably healthy, however, you can skip this aeration.

Old-timers swore by top-dressings carefully compounded of all sorts of ingredients: sand, loam, and ashes, and so on, as well as the organic matter. We, by contrast, never use anything but pure compost, and we sprinkle it in a layer up to ¼-inch thick. That's a lot of compost: it took just about a full bin's-worth to treat Tom's tiny, 50 × 40-foot front yard. If your lawn measures a princely half acre (better you should mow it than us), then clearly it can consume every bit of compost you can produce; to cover it to a uniform depth of ¼ inch would take the contents of 17 bins, if each one held the standard cubic yard.

We realize that spreading so much compost is probably more work than you care to undertake. That's OK; top-dressing needn't be an all-or-nothing proposition. If you apply a thinner top-dressing, it may not supply all the nutrients the grass needs for healthy growth, but it will reduce the lawn's appetite for fertilizers. As little as 10 pounds of compost per 1,000 square feet will give effective protection from harmful fungi. Best of all, in

FIGURE 11. Compost lawn-care: top-dressing is an old-time ▶ greenskeeper's trick, one whose time has come again. A quarter-inch of compost in both spring and fall should provide your grass with all the nutrients it needs without polluting the groundwater or nearby streams with chemical run-off. Top-dressings with homemade compost will also leave the lawn more drought-resistant, and disease-resistant, too.

1. If the lawn is thin or mossy, use a gas-powered aerator (a day's rental will cost around $50.00) to punch cores out of the turf and allow air and water better access to grass roots.

2. Next spread the compost (home-made is best, but the commercially produced kind is o.k., too) in a 1/4-inch-deep layer; that's 2 cubic feet of compost (7 1/2 2-gallon-bucket-fulls) per 100 square feet of lawn.

3. Rake lawn to break up aerator's cores, spread compost more evenly and remove twigs and other un-decomposed compostables. Schedule the top-dressing for mid-fall and you can save work by combining this with routine leaf removal.

the matter of water conservation, the effect of the applications is cumulative. Several years of meager top-dressings can together substantially alter your soil's composition, significantly adding to its organic content, and making it a better reservoir for rainwater.

Turf maintenance manuals insist that only sifted compost—compost that has been passed through a screen to remove lumps and twigs—may be used for top-dressing. Shaking a cubic yard of compost through a screen, however, is too much work even for Tom, and it's fortunate that this operation really isn't as necessary as the experts maintain. When we top-dress, we load the compost straight from the bin into the wheelbarrow and then sling it about the lawn by the shovelful. Afterward we give the lawn a thorough going over with a spring rake. That distributes the compost more evenly and removes any large debris, and since we top-dress in midfall, it doesn't involve any extra work, because we'd be raking the lawn anyway to remove the fallen leaves.

Research for this book brought about an enormous increase in compost production in our yards—but a switch to compost lawn care gave us a use for all we could produce. And while our lawns still don't match the velvety green carpets you see on the packages of lawn care chemicals, they look fine—and they aren't poisoning us or the neighbors.

2. New Lawns

The amount of organic matter you should mix with the soil before sowing a new lawn depends on the soil's condition—a complete soil test (available inexpensively through the local office of the Cooperative Extension Service) will provide exact recommendations. The landscaper's rule of thumb, though, is 3 cubic yards of compost per 1,000 square feet—rake it out into an even

blanket and mix it in to a depth of 6 inches with a ro-
totiller.

3. Flower Gardens and Vegetable Beds

We've already examined the ways that compost can
benefit these plants, and we needn't go into that again.
But given that you should add compost to the beds, how
much is enough?

That depends partly on the soil. A really poor, sandy
soil requires an extra big dose, since without compost
it cannot retain either water or nutrients. A sticky clay
soil will also require extra compost, since compost will
help lighten the soil, breaking it up into crumbs so that
air and water can penetrate. A good loam will require
less compost, since it already contains substantial
amounts of organic material. In general, though, an average level you should aim at is 5 percent. That is, humus should compose 5 percent (by weight) of the total
soil.

That may not sound like much organic matter, but
in fact it amounts to about 100,000 pounds per acre in
the top 6 inches of soil alone. If you follow the recommendation you find in your gardening books and
double-dig your beds—that is, turn the soil to a depth
of two bites of the spade—you'll need even more compost. In that case, we suggest that you spread the compost over the whole bed in an inch-deep layer before
you set spade to soil.

Not all this compost will remain in the soil as humus. The soil's microflora will fairly rapidly consume a
substantial fraction, which will then be released to the
plants as nutrients. Even compost that does stabilize as
humus is not a truly permanent addition. As noted in
Chapter 4 the decomposition continues, albeit at a
slower rate. The rate of this degradation depends in

large part on your skill as a gardener. A well-managed bed—one that is properly fertilized, aerated, and watered—is an ideal environment for microflora as well as garden plants, and the humus is consumed there more quickly.

Even Tom can't be bothered with continual testing of his garden beds, but he has found that an application of another inch of humus every year keeps his beds in good condition. Because the area of his beds totals about 200 square feet, feeding them in this fashion requires about two-thirds of a cubic yard of compost annually, or two-thirds of a binfull.

4. Water Conservation

We've already discussed the way that compost can boost a soil's ability to absorb and retain water (see Chapter 4). Because reducing water use is such an important concern in many parts of the country (from south Florida to the Southwest and even many midwestern regions), we thought we ought to include specific recommendations.

Experts in water-conserving gardening ("xeriscapers" as they sometimes call themselves) generally recommend adding to each new planting area a dose of compost equal to a fourth of the soil's volume. That is, if you are spading up a new flower bed and intend to dig the soil to a depth of 10 inches (a depth equal to the spade's blade) first cover the area with a layer of compost 2½ inches deep. Better yet, dig the soil to a depth of *two* spades (20 inches) and add 5 inches of compost. In either case, make sure to blend the compost thoroughly; after breaking the soil with the spade, turn it with a spading fork.

The effect of this treatment will vary with the quality of your compost, and your soil type, but usually the effect is dramatic. A fine-particled but purely mineral soil such as a silt or clay may absorb and hold an amount of water equal to 45 percent of its dry weight—but a really humus-rich soil, like the black, crumbly material you scrape up from the forest floor, will retain roughly six to ten times more. That means a compost-enriched soil will provide a far more capacious reservoir for your plants. It will absorb much more of whatever rain that falls, letting far less of this moisture escape as runoff, and that reduces the amount of water you must provide. Likewise, the compost-enriched soil will absorb and retain much more efficiently any water you apply with the hose, so that you must water far less often. Besides, most plants grow better on a water-retentive soil—the cycle of drought–soak–drought you get with organic-poor soils is especially destructive to vegetables, reducing both the quantity and quality of the harvest.

5. House Plants

If you've ever made the mistake of planting your house plants into a potful of ordinary garden soil, you know that doesn't work. Conditions in a 6-inch clay pot are very different from those in a garden bed, and the same soil that performs well outdoors soon subsides into a muddy concrete indoors. House plants must survive in unnatural conditions, and the type of soil they require is artificial. To make a good potting mix, you must add a couple of things to the soil but the key is extra organic matter—compost.

Of course, you may decide it's easier just to buy your potting soil already mixed and bagged at the garden center. But that's a pig in a poke in every sense. Bagged potting soils rarely list their ingredients, and what they contain varies wildly. We've bought some that were clearly nothing but black silt poured into a sack, and there are many others that actually contain no real soil at all. These so-called soils are blends of everything from expanded mica to peanut shells and styrofoam. Your plants may tolerate that, but we believe they'd be happier with earth. Certainly we are.

Plants can be as difficult as people, and according to the old Italians who taught Tom to garden, almost every species preferred a somewhat different potting mix. Tom was never able to keep straight all the different menus, however, so he pots all of his plants into one of three different formulas. Sand, soil, and compost are the basic ingredients of each.

The soil may be any good garden soil—if you don't like what you find in the backyard, you can buy a bag of topsoil at the garden center. The sand must be coarse and abrasive—a "sharp" sand, is what masons call it, and Tom buys it in bags at building supply outlets. Sandbox sand is an acceptable substitute, but stay away from beach sand—the action of the waves has rounded off its corners so that the grains pack together too tightly. The compost comes from Tom's bin and when he's using it for potting soil he does sift it—the screen he uses for this he made by stapling a piece of ¼-inch metal mesh ("hardware cloth" is what it's sold as) across a bottomless wooden box.

For most plants, Tom uses a blend of one part soil to one part sand and one part compost. For plants such as African violets, begonias, or ferns, those for which the handbooks recommend an "organic" potting mix, Tom boosts the amount of compost, mixing two parts soil with three parts compost and one-half part sand. For cacti and other dry land plants, Tom increases the sand: one part soil, one part compost, and two parts sand. If the handbook specifies a "limey," or alkaline, soil, Tom crushes a couple of eggshells and adds them to the pot.

Gardening guides often recommend heat-treating your potting mix to kill any harmful bugs or microorganisms that may have slipped in with the soil. You can do that by putting it in a baking pan, burying a potato in it, and keeping it in a 350-degree oven until the potato is cooked. This process smells awful, though, and it kills good microorganisms along with the bad. Our experience is that it's unnecessary; the high proportion of compost in our mixes seems to provide adequate protection against pathogens.

Since new seedlings are especially vulnerable, however, we do suggest that you start seeds in a commercially produced "peat-lite" mix, a sterile potting medium composed of an inert grit and sphagnum peat. By the time the seedlings have developed two true leaves and are ready for transplanting to individual pots, they will be sufficiently mature that you may plant them into the appropriate one of our three basic formulas.

That's what Tom does with his compost, and it's clear why he can't make enough of it. With Marty, it's a different story. Although he lives in a suburb now, he only recently left the city and he's still a boulevardier at heart. A grudging acceptance of frozen bagels is about the extent of his adjustment to country living, and he composts mainly because his daughter Madeleine insists. She has been greening his habits ever since she caught him dropping a candy wrapper on a Manhattan street corner, and the heap is a required part of the course.

Marty doesn't dislike gardening. On the contrary, he admires it very much — mostly from a distance. He is conscientious about lawn care, but other than that his personal horticultural activities are limited mostly to a couple of tomato vines. Still, he finds compost comes in handy.

It's a wonderful tonic for the croquet lawn. Sift it

into the hollows, adding another ¼-inch layer every month or so, and in one season it will bring the turf to that perfect level a serious player demands.

It gives a special flavor to his tomatoes, he believes, and Marty hopes that those fruits will endow him with a special vigor. He read a report by the leading physician of British India's northwest frontier, Sir Robert Mc-Carrison (and you better believe he made house calls), about the superb health of his patients, the Hunza people of Kashmir. This condition is not simply a result of climate, for the Hunzas' nearest neighbors, the Ishkominas, McCarrison revealed, are "poor, undersized and under-nourished creatures." Those fools burn their refuse and animal manures. But the Hunzas, they compost everything that isn't nailed down. The immeasurably superior vegetables this produces allow the Hunzas to flourish completely free of dyspepsia, appendicitis, cancer, and (this is of greatest interest to an editor such as Marty) without gastric *or* duodenal ulcers.[2]

And then there is the best use Marty has found for his compost: it pleases Madeleine.

Energy from Compost

For at least one of composting's benefits, you don't even have to wait until the heap cools. Indeed, if you wait that long, you will have missed it.

The benefit we have in mind is the energy you can harvest from your compost heap. Composting is a series of chemical reactions, and most of the energy it produces is gobbled up by the decomposers. But some es-

---

[2] W. E. Shewell-Cooper, *Compost Gardening,* David & Charles (Newton Abbot, UK, 1972), p. 26.

capes as by-products and waste heat, and the BTUs contained in these are considerable.

In Belgium, for example, they are using a form of composting to produce natural gas. Solid waste is shredded, mixed, and heated, and then sealed into an enormous drum, or "digester." For the next eighteen days, as anaerobic decomposers break down the waste, it releases daily a volume of methane equal to six or eight times the volume of the digester. Afterward the solid residue is further composted to produce a high-quality soil amendment.

There are corporate farms in the United States that are using a similar process to turn manures into electricity. But that requires an infrastructure beyond our means. Every time the home heating bill comes due, though, Tom recalls a successful experiment conducted by one of his gardening mentors—John Albert of the New York Botanical Garden.

That institution is located in the Bronx, an area that the world perceives as a wasteland. John, however, knew it as a borough of great and unexploited natural resources, and it was his genius to tap into one of the most massive of these: elephant manure. Every month during the winter of 1976–1977, John would cross the street to the Bronx Zoo and pick up a dumptruckload of fresh dung from the elephant house and take it back to dump it in a drum he had made by bolting together three pieces of 4 × 8-foot sheet metal. Then he'd cover the drum with a plywood cap and turn on a squirrel fan in the adjacent greenhouse.

The fan sucked air and steam from the composting manure into his greenhouse, where it circulated through a crude radiator made of stovepipe. The heat released in this way was sufficient to heat the greenhouse, while the carbon dioxide that the composting manure released enhanced the growth of John's plants.

Another effect of this system was to continuously aerate the composting manure—by drawing air out from the top of the drum John created a partial vacuum that in turn pulled air in through an intake at the base of the drum's wall and up through its contents.

One fill-up of manure was sufficient to heat John's greenhouse for a month. As the heat dropped at the end of that period, John knew the compost inside the drum was garden ready, and he'd remove and replace it. That's what really appeals to us, or at least to Tom: a pretext to add 5 *cubic yards* of finished compost to his supply every month, all winter long. What a way to get ready for spring!

Compost Cookery

The medium may be the message, but often it's the flavor too. It's no accident that Hoboken, New Jersey, is the North American capital for Italian bread lovers—the coal-fired brick oven at *Marie's Bakery* endows its huge, round loaves with the perfect contrast of brittle crust and chewy, moist interior. And anyone who has tasted real Texas barbecue and then been disappointed by counterfeits knows that it is the Texans' mesquite-fired pits that make the difference. Tom knows these things. That's why he had high hopes for compost cookery.

Through his browsing in old compost manuals, he had learned that cooking with the heap is an old Chinese custom. Presumably, between inventing the printing press and gunpowder and trying to civilize Marco Polo, some Chinese had time to notice that his compost heap was really hot, and decided to take advantage of the phenomenon. Or maybe times were tough, and some poor soul was rooting through a rich neighbor's compost heap in search of an old winter melon or a discarded sea slug and found them—wonder of wonders—cooked to a turn.

However compost cookery began, the Chinese have since elevated it to high art; unfortunately, neither Tom nor Marty can read the relevant cookbooks. This didn't disturb Marty, whose response to this particular project was wholly negative — his contribution, he said, would be to take Tom's wife out to dinner on the night that the compost cooking was served. That didn't deter Tom, who was certain he could recreate this ancient art on his own.

In the interest of hygiene, he forwent his usual composting stand-by — fresh horse manure — and this time charged the heap with shredded leaves, cotton-seed meal, a few cups of 5–10–5 fertilizer, and kitchen scraps. Whereupon he discovered one of the disadvantages of compost cookery: that night the weather turned cold and the heap froze solid. This of course put the project on hold — Tom's meal was delayed until the cold snap ended, a full month.

As soon as spring returned, Tom forked up the heap to aerate the compostables and within a couple of days it was steaming hot. Tom bathed a couple of chicken thighs in a marinade of soy sauce, sherry, garlic, ginger, coriander, and black pepper, and then sealed them in a Zip-Lock plastic bag. After sealing this first bag inside another plastic bag, he buried the whole in the heart of the hot heap.

About twenty-four hours later he exhumed the dish and extracted the chicken. It looked . . . OK. The chicken thighs had a sort of pale look to them, but no worse than what you get from microwave cooking — apparently a heap is of no use for browning. But when Tom sliced into the meat with a sharp knife, he found that the chicken had the texture of cooked meat and that it seemed wonderfully moist. Making sure that he had the telephone number of the poison control center handy, Tom then sat down to a lonely dinner.

He cut and ate a scrap but couldn't really taste it —

thoughts of salmonella were crowding so boisterously into his head that they blocked all sensation from the taste buds. What good would it do to savor the chicken, Tom rationalized, if he didn't live to record the experience? So he cheated a little, and microwaved one chicken thigh for three minutes at his oven's highest setting. Then he returned it—bacteria-free now, he trusted—to the table.

Sure enough, the chicken *did* have a distinctive flavor. It was earthy—in fact, it tasted just like a compost heap smells. Tom really likes that smell out in the garden, but he discovered that it doesn't translate well to the dining room. He stuck it out through a whole thigh, but then tossed the rest, marinade and all, into his Green Cone.

Tom's first thought was that he must have done something wrong. Maybe he should have somehow adjusted the setting on the heap—had he been cooking on high when he should have kept the compostables at a simmer? Should he have used yet a third plastic bag? Did the chicken need a pinch more garlic? But on reflection Tom has decided that the problem was more likely in his occidental taste buds than in the chicken. That time his Taiwanese friend introduced him to sea slugs, Tom found repellent a dish that she obviously relished. It must be an acquired taste. Tom believes that he should give compost cookery another chance. Only next time he gets to go out with Marty while Suzanne stays home to dig into the organically steamed goody.

CHAPTER 9

Community Composting

E PLURIBUS UNUM —"From many, one"—that's the American way, and this motto applies just as surely to composting as to government. For how are we going to get all the compost we need, the billions and trillions of tons, without collective action? We need to join heap to heap, we need whole communities composting together.

Even Tom recognizes this. He may enjoy processing his own garbage, but he has to admit that many of his neighbors do not. Sometimes he even wonders about Marty. Anyway, Tom realizes that there is a lot of compost that never will get made unless the government undertakes to do it for us.

We need trucks to pick up the organic garbage and haul it off to concrete-block buildings with time clocks for the workers and coffee machines for executives. We need giant machines to shred and turn the compostables, to sift the compost when it is done, and stuff it into bags. We need systems and programs, computer inventories, and a five-year plan. In short, we need an industry.

We are getting one, too. As of this writing (March 1993), there were already some 1,500 community leaf-and-yard-waste composting programs. Composting municipal solid waste (MSW) is off to a slower but still solid start. There were twenty-one plants processing, with sixty-one more in some stage of development. All over the country, men and women are putting on polyester overalls to report in to the new compost plant—Al Gore wasn't kidding when he said that environmentalism would produce more jobs.

In most cases, the composting programs have proved to be a good thing. But before you rush off to your broker to float a bond issue, read on a few pages and make sure that what you build will be an asset to your community. Because among the successes there have been some spectacular failures. Consider, for example, what happened at the Agripost plant in Dade County, Florida.

This facility had inspired high hopes—it was to process 800 tons of mixed solid waste per day—and it would turn this dross into agricultural gold, compost that would supply the needs of South Florida's humus-hungry nurseries, landscapers, and farmers. The actual result, though, was that despite an investment of $26 million[1] the plant never operated at full capacity, and that in May 1991, twenty months after the arrival of the first garbage truck, it closed its gates forever.

---

[1] That's precisely twice the average cost of building an MSW composting plant.

It was a victim of wishful thinking.

To begin with, both voters and their elected officials viewed composting as a panacea. It was going to save them so much money—they were counting the returns from compost sales before the first brick was laid at the plant, and no one ever thought to investigate whether there really would be a market, and what kind of compost the buyers would want. Compost is good, it's natural, and everybody likes that. What could go wrong?

Smell? The engineers who were designing the plant assured everyone that properly aerated compost didn't smell. So they didn't take precautions to ensure that any odor generated in the composting process could be contained. Even if they had wanted to, though, they couldn't have afforded any such equipment, because Dade County was intent on doing its composting on the cheap.

It contracted the construction and management of the plant to a private corporation, Agripost, and left the contractor the problem of finding the necessary funds. Then it refused to pay Agripost a tipping fee (a per-ton fee for dumping trash at the plant) that would provide an adequate income. Dade County had long enjoyed landfill costs a fraction of those of its neighbors—Dade haulers pay about half as much as their competitors in the county immediately to the north and little more than a third as much as those in the county to the south. Rather than tell the electorate it would have to pay more for trash removal, the politicians relied on an economy of scale. They insisted on a plant whose costs would be low because of the immense amount of garbage it would handle.

Raising the stakes in that fashion ensured that any bugs in the system would produce not problems but disasters. At the same time, the low tipping fees made bankers unwilling to provide all the money that Agripost needed, so it had to cut more corners in equipping the plant. For example, the machinery it installed to screen the finished compost, preparing it for sale, couldn't handle more than a fourth of the plant's intended output, and so the compost piled up around the perimeter of the plant in violation of state regulations. Not that it mattered. Agripost had avoided the bother of state testing and inspection of its product by claiming that its operation preceded the state's establishment of those regulations — only to find that customers were afraid of a product that *could* be (who could tell?) contaminated.

The death blow, though, was the odors associated with the plant. Snags did develop in the processing in the startup stages, and at times a stink did crawl out of the plant. Residents of adjacent neighborhoods complained, and though Agripost began installing systems to contain the problem, it was too late. Because by then neighbors were blaming the compost plant for every bad smell that wafted in through their windows. There were plenty of those, too, since the county, in working on the adjacent landfill, was exhuming 350,000 cubic yards of decade-old garbage that first summer. Eventually a hearing was held in which the star performer was the principal of a nearby elementary school, who brought fifty pupils to complain (without any corroborative evidence) of the "acid dust" that was poisoning the student body. That was when the politicians ran for cover and closed the plant.

Who was at fault? Nearly everyone involved. Who suffered? Everyone from the contractor—who went bankrupt—to county taxpayers whose landfill will have a shorter life span (because it must handle garbage that could be composted) and who will eventually have to find a new solution to waste disposal anyway.

What could Dade County have done to avoid this

mess? It could have sent someone across the country to visit Seattle, Washington. Seattle provides a fine example of what a well-conceived and well-managed community composting program can achieve.

Seattle started composting because, unlike Dade County, it had no cheap rooms at the landfill. In fact, by 1985 it had hardly any space at all. It had already closed one landfill and the remaining one was due to close the following year. Both were classified as Superfund sites, and it was going to cost the city $96 million to put them to rest. That was one reason why Seattle was reluctant to switch to incineration—no one liked the idea of spreading more toxins around. Anyhow, after looking at the figures, the Solid Waste Utility realized that it would be cheaper to eliminate most of the trash at the source through recycling, compost what it could of the rest, and pay to haul the remaining fraction to someone else's landfill. But the Solid Waste Utility realized that it was going to take more than arithmetic to make this work.

Seattle didn't want to commit itself to any one option before it was sure the measure would work. That's why the Solid Waste Utility chose to work through a team of consultants, private organizations, and nonprofit groups. This gave the Solid Waste Utility a maximum of flexibility—if a trial project didn't work out, then termination was just a matter of stopping the funding, not layoffs of city workers. So the Solid Waste Utility took care to educate itself before plunging into composting. But more important, it educated citizens.

Indeed, the Utility spent four years (1985–1989) on public education before it actually began composting. To help in this, moreover, it tapped the very considerable experience of Seattle Tilth. A nonprofit organization dedicated to the promotion of ecologically sound gardening and agriculture, Seattle Tilth had lots of experience in both composting and public outreach, and for the new Community Composting Education Program it came up with an idea that has had nationwide effect. The "Master Composter" program it designed has proven such a success in Seattle that it has since been copied by a hundred or more other communities.[2]

Briefly, Master Composters are volunteers who are willing to commit at least 100 hours to promoting this form of waste reduction. The first 36 hours they spend on classroom, field trip, and hands-on training in the art and science of composting, and the next 24 hours they devote to an internship, working with the instructors or graduates. Finally, having graduated, the newly minted masters each spend 40 more hours on community outreach. This may take the form of manning compost demonstration sites where passers-by can inspect a dozen different methods of composting in operation (choose the style that suits *you*). Master Composters distribute free literature on the how-to's and benefits of composting; they staff the compost hotline that residents with a problem can call; and they make house calls, providing onsite instruction at the composter-to-be's own home.

These volunteers have brought not only enthusiasm to the educational campaign, but also added impact. Speaking as ordinary residents, householder to house-

---

[2]Seattle Tilth shares program materials with interested community groups, and will even send out members to consult and help set up local composting and recycling programs. Because of the numbers of requests it receives and its limited resources, Seattle Tilth will not respond to requests by private individuals seeking information for personal use. For information about programs and fees, write to Seattle Tilth Association at 4649 Sunnyside Avenue North, Seattle, Washington 98103, and include $2 and a legal-sized, self-addressed, stamped envelope.

holder, Master Composters have a credibility that no public relations mouthpiece could have. In addition, the Master Composters have provided a vital entree into the ethnic neighborhoods on Seattle's south side. When it became clear that the composting message wasn't penetrating there, Seattle Tilth began visiting street fairs and other community celebrations to enroll local residents in the Master Composter program. Then it helped these recruits reinterpret the composting programs for their neighbors, sponsoring, for example, demonstration sites at a community center and a neighborhood garden.

By including so many different voices, Seattle helped to make composting truly the people's choice, and has prevented the emergence of a not-in-my-backyard movement of the kind that swept Dade County. Which was essential, since that is precisely where Seattle's Solid Waste Utility intended to do its composting.

Rather than building a Stalinist megaplant, in 1989 the Utility began encouraging residents to start composting themselves by distributing free bins. Initially these were made of cedar wood slats, until someone realized that this could be an outlet for all the recycled plastic the city was collecting—now the bins are made of perforated plastic sheets, and to date 25,000 have been distributed. Thanks to Seattle Tilth's educational pump priming, citizen cooperation has been excellent.

To avoid rodent problems, the utility has recommended that the bins be used only for yard wastes—surveys have revealed that 70 percent of bin recipients do compost and that each composter processes on average 70 percent of the organic waste his or her yard generates. That means the bin distribution program has kept off the streets about 50 percent—on average 260 pounds per year—of the grass clippings, hedge trimmings, and tree leaves from 25,000 yards.

Not bad. And for those who don't want to compost at home, the city will (for a fee of $3 per month) haul yard wastes to a site thirty miles outside city limits where a private contractor mass composts the debris. The Solid Waste Utility's contribution to this program has been a vigorous marketing campaign that includes display gardens of crops grown with the municipal compost. Since yard wastes don't typically include the kinds of dangerous contaminants that may be found in the catch-all of mixed solid waste, the sale has been an easy one. The contractor is selling compost as fast as it can process it—50,000 cubic yards in the first year of operation alone.

The Solid Waste Utility intends to distribute another 45,000 yard waste bins, and with the success of that program it was (as of 1993) eyeing kitchen waste. To help residents compost that, it would distribute separate, more rodent-proof systems, letting recipients choose between a worm bin and a Green Cone. Kitchen waste, utility spokesman Carl Woestwin noted, contributes only 0.6 percent of Seattle's total solid waste stream. But add that to the 55,000 tons of yard waste composted annually by the city contractors and the 3,250 tons composted in backyard bins, and you have a substantial fraction of the 60 percent waste reduction that is Seattle's goal for the year 1998. That's an ambitious target, but combine the composting with a recycling program that enjoys 80 percent compliance, and the Seattle city fathers and mothers are confident they will reach it.

By tailoring its composting program, Seattle has managed to sidestep a number of the problems that plague many other municipal composters. But circumstances may prevent your community from following Seattle's blueprint; you may lack the resources, or your interest in composting may be the result of a special waste problem that you *must* address. Therefore, it's worth looking at how you can confront those difficulties successfully.

To begin with, any bulk composter must plan for odor control. Managing a backyard heap so that it remains essentially odor free is easy; doing the same with hundreds of tons of wastes a day is not. Seattle avoided this situation by siting its bulk composting operation well outside city limits, and has avoided attacking the nitrogen-rich, wet, and potentially stinky, mixed waste—garbage. But a garbage disposal problem may be precisely why your community is interested in composting, and anyway, even restricting your activities to yard waste is no guarantee that a plant will remain odor free.

Any program that handles large amounts of fresh grass clippings, for example, can expect to experience odor problems in warm weather. Gases with such self-explanatory names as "cadaverine" will develop no matter what the composter does—and that's because they will develop before the clippings ever reach the composting plant. Once sealed in a plastic bag and set out on a sunny curb, juicy fresh clippings start composting before the town truck can come by to pick them up, and the type of composting they pursue is the anaerobic, odoriferous kind. So the compostables arrive already equipped with a stink, and merely opening the bags may outrage neighbors.

Immediately mixing the clippings (or any other incoming high-nitrogen material) with abundant quantities of some carbon source such as dry leaves (at a rate of two or three parts leaves to one part grass) will help stop the gas generation. That may be a sufficient safeguard for a rurally situated plant. For composting plants in populated areas, however, a better solution may be to open all bags of compostables inside a closed building equipped with some sort of air filtration and cleansing system. One of the most effective devices of this kind — and definitely the most ecologically friendly — is what is known as a "biofilter."

A biofilter is really just another kind of recycling. It begins with a system of exhaust fans that continually draw air out of the composting building; the air is then fed into a network of ducts and finally pushed up through a bed of gravel topped with several feet of mature compost, a layer of peat, and a layer of leaves. These three upper layers host innumerable decomposers, and they devour the passing gases (which are, after all, just leftovers from an incomplete decomposition) breaking them down to simpler and less pungent compounds. As the great Pogo once observed, one man's obscenity is another man's lunch.

Actually, any large-scale composting operation that handles high-nitrogen materials such as grass clippings will probably at the least generate ammonia (a nitrogen waste product). That's why so-called in-vessel composting systems are becoming increasingly popular. These pack the organic wastes into enclosed bays equipped with mechanical devices for churning and aerating the compostables. Such systems are relatively easy to equip with a biofilter, or with some other system such as sprinklers that periodically mist the degrading compostables with chemical "neutralizers" (guess which option we prefer?).

Often odors result from a problem with the fundamental design of the composting system itself — the pad on which the compostables are mixed and stacked, for example, may not drain sufficiently well, so that the compost tends to stay wet and anaerobic. Such problems can be corrected, but if the plant designers have made no provision for containing the stench in the meantime, the solution may come too late. Once put the idea in neighbors' heads that the composting plant smells like a dump, and you will probably never manage to soften their hostility.

We had thought that community composting was a brand new trend, but when we took the time to do some reading, we learned that in fact cities in California, Arizona, Oklahoma, Alabama, and Florida began building pilot projects as early as the mid 1950s. So the process isn't in its infancy. But it's not a mature technology yet either—it's still developing and changing as engineers and scientists test new techniques and new solutions. That's why creating a successful program demands flexibility. To a degree, most composting communities find they must make up their own solutions as they go along. This is especially true if (as is often so) your town faces an uncommon situation.

Take the case of Mackinac Island, Michigan. The special attraction this resort commnunity offers visitors is its quiet, rural lifestyle—and to ensure this, the community has banned all motor traffic from the island. Once you disembark from the ferry, you travel by horse-drawn carriage. That means the Mackinackers don't suffer from engine noise or exhaust fumes. But they do collect lots of manure. How much? Bill Smith, the deputy director of Public Works, wasn't sure, but he knows there are 300 to 400 horses trotting around the island in summertime, so what we are discussing is *tons*.

This used to be a problem. Waste removal is expensive on Mackinac—whatever the material, it has to be collected with horse-drawn drays, and then packed out to landfills via the ferry. In 1992, though, the Department of Public Works realized that the manure could bea resource as well. It was an ideal material with which to enrich the organic fraction of the residents' garbage and yard wastes; this hearty blend would compost with a minimum of treatment.

What's the Waste	What's the Problem
UNDER THE KITCHEN SINK Floor & Furniture polishes	May contain various petroleum distillates and other chemicals that with prolonged exposure can damage liver or kidneys, cause cancer.
Ammonia	Can burn skin or eyes, irritate lungs.
IN THE BATHROOM Disinfectants, tub and tile cleaners	May contain solvents and other chemicals that with prolonged exposure may cause liver and kidney damage, or cancer.
Nail polish and polish remover	Contains formaldehyde, implicated as a carcinogen, and various toxic solvents: acetone, toluene, etc.
Medicines	
IN THE BASEMENT Oil-based paints and stains	Various hydrocarbons, petroleum distillates, fungicides, ethylene. Exposure can cause headache, nausea, liver and kidney damage, birth defects, etc.
Wood preservatives	May contain carcinogens such as creosote and arsenic.
Thinners and strippers	Toxic solvents such as acetone and toluene, petroleum distillates.
IN THE GARAGE Pesticides, fungicides, weed-killers	Many highly toxic, water-soluble and some extremely persistent.
Motor oil	Every year home auto mechanics spill more oil into the waterways (via storm drains) than all the tanker accidents. Besides the toxicity of the petroleum, used motor oil contains traces of heavy metals such as lead and cadmium.
AND ELSEWHERE Batteries	Source of most heavy metals (lead, cadmium, mercury, etc.) in household garbage.
Mothballs	Active principal, paradichlorobenzene, toxic to people and wildlife as well as moths. Prolonged exposure can cause damage to kidneys and liver.

FIGURE 12. Hazardous waste. Your household produces an average of 15 lbs. of this every year.

Safe Disposal

Contact local Cooperative Extension Office or State Department of Environmental Protection for information about community hazardous waste collection programs.

Dilute with water and pour down drain (take care not to overload septic system, if any). Or dilute with water (1/4 cup ammonia to 1 gallon water) and use to moisten compost heap.

Dilute with water and pour down drain (do not overload septic system, if any) or save for community hazardous waste collection program.

Mix nail polish with absorbent material such as kitty litter, let dry, double-wrap in plastic and dispose of with garbage. Save nail polish remover for community hazardous waste collection program.

Contact physician or pharmacist. Generally safe to dispose of (diluted with water) down drain.

Save for community hazardous waste collection program.

Save for community hazardous waste collection program.

Save for community hazardous waste collection program.

Save for community hazardous waste collection program.

Recycle at local service station or contact Cooperative Extension or Department of Environmental Protection about local recycling programs.

Special recycling programs exist in some areas - contact local Cooperative Extension or save for community hazardous waste collection programs.

Save for community hazardous waste collection program.

The best way to handle such hazardous materials is, of course, to buy only what you need and use it up, or to switch to less toxic alternatives. Information about these is commonly available from the local Department of Health or Cooperative Extension. In any case, always read and observe warnings and instructions on the product label.

(See "Resources" for more information.)

The process the town has adopted is effective, but also remarkably simple. First, all wastes are shredded in a big tub grinder, then they are screened and dumped in 50×50-foot bays equipped with a system for forcing air up through the piles. Once there, the wastes just sit, for four months. After that, they are scooped up and stacked outside in windrows.

This is only a short step from Marty's Uriah Heap — yet Bill Smith figures that Mackinac is disposing of 65 to 70 percent of its nonrecyclable waste in this fashion. That's 8 tons per day in the peak tourist season.

The road to successful composting does not always run smooth, however, and the island's first season (1992) ended in failure. On the advice of an engineering firm the community tried to process mixed waste. That is, everything that went into the residents' trash also went into the compost, with the assumption that contaminants could be screened out when decay had reduced the organic fraction to crumbs. In the event, what this thinking produced was 300 cubic yards of compost so thoroughly contaminated with shredded plastic that Mackinac couldn't give it away—it had to send it to the landfill. So the town fired the engineers and switched to "source separation."

Source separation means that garbage is sorted into three fractions — compostables, recyclables, and those things that are neither—and the sorting is done up front by the producers (you and me). Then the one bag goes to the recycling plant, another goes to the landfill and the incinerator, while the third lands with a bump on the floor of the compost plant. That may not seem like a revolutionary concept—but the fact is that this type of do-it-yourself treatment runs directly contrary to a century of waste management.

Our ideals in that matter have been based on the characteristic American passions for technology, hygiene, and convenience. Garbage in America goes as quickly as possible into sealed plastic bags so that it can then disappear down the highway in a truck. If handling should become necessary, if a desire to compost should dictate sorting wastes according to type, well then, we'll build a machine. With considerable ingenuity, we've combined mechanized sifters with jets of air, banks of magnets, and electrical systems that can make a can leap off a conveyor belt and into a hopper *by itself.* And when someone has dared to point out that it works better to sort garbage by hand back in the kitchen, the sanitary engineers have replied that Americans won't tolerate the inconvenience of source separation, or the expense of running two or even three collection trucks along each route.

We may have to, though, if we don't want to drown in garbage. Because even the most sophisticated centralized sorting systems suffer from three serious problems.

To begin with, there is a limit to the machine's powers of discrimination. Small bits of glass and plastic have a way of slipping through (as Mackinac Island discovered) to make the finished compost unsightly and unsalable, if not actually hazardous. Then, too, environmentalists complain that the mechanized sorting systems encourage waste. Forcing compost plants to accept mixed wastes turns them into Dispose-Alls, garbage gobblers that devour large amounts of potentially recyclable materials such as waste paper.

That's inefficient. Although composting may foster the regrowth of forests, recycling paper reduces the need to cut them in the first place. Even those more durable recyclables, such as aluminum cans, that the separation mechanisms do collect often end up so soiled as to be virtually worthless. This is why the state of Texas, which has adopted the EPA's goal of reducing or recycling 40 percent of the waste stream by the end of the century, will not accept mixed-waste composting as a part of this effort.

Not that source separation entirely eliminates either of these problems. Even concerned householders have careless moments and on Mackinac Island, workers still have to pick through the incoming waste to remove contaminants. Upon opening the trash bags, they give the contents a quick visual inspection, remove any obvious problems, and then kick the rest down a chute and onto a conveyor that runs the waste past more human pickers and under a magnet that pulls out any iron or steel. Clearly, source separation doesn't provide a complete cure for the problem of contaminants, but the experience in plants such as Mackinac's is that source separation can reduce their amount by a factor of 10 or more.

Source separation's most important role in municipal waste composting, though, has to do with a third problem, and that is hazardous wastes. When we asked Bill Smith about the level of such toxins in Mackinac's garbage, he dismissed our question with the explanation that there is no industry on the island. This reflects a common misconception, that the hazardous waste in our trash all originates in factories.

The fact is that the average American household generates about 15 pounds of hazardous waste a year — and what doesn't go down the drain generally ends up in the trash. Batteries contribute heavy metals such as lead, nickel, cadmium, zinc, copper, and mercury to this flow; cleaning products, polishes, and paints add solvents; and the dangers of the half-empty bottles of pesticides you sneak out with the trash are obvious. Some other items aren't. The Walkman you toss into the trash, for instance: consumer electronics equipment accounts for 27 percent of the lead in the residential waste stream. Roughly 25 percent of the cadmium comes from pigments and stabilizers used in plastics. And if the quantities added in this fashion seem negligible, think again: one standard C-size battery contains more than 4,000 times what federal guidelines have established as the maximum allowable daily dose of mercury.

Many of the organic solvents and petroleum products will break down during the composting process, but some—notably the fungicides we buy to spread on our lawns—degrade into carcinogens. Other toxins, notably the heavy metals, survive composting intact. Indeed, as the composting process reduces the weight and bulk of the waste, it works to concentrate the hazardous wastes, meaning that the resulting compost may smell and look healthful and yet be half again as toxic as the original truckload of repulsive trash.

Worse yet, composting can concentrate these toxins in another way. As the compost we have spread over our landscape decays, we may repeat the treatment once, twice, or many times. But if the compost decays, many of the toxins (the heavy metals in particular) do not. So we periodically add another dose of lead, cadmium, zinc, asbestos, and others, gradually making our farms and parks more and more like landfills.

To be fair, we should stress that generally composts must meet federal or state safety standards if they are to be used in such sensitive areas. The baseline for these standards is the toxin levels that the EPA has established as NOAELs: *n*o-*o*bservable-*a*dverse-*e*ffects-*l*evels. These standards apply to *all* composts made from sewage sludge (which ironically makes them among the safest of municipally produced composts) and are commonly the foundation for the state standards that govern municipal solid waste composts. State standards vary, however; some states have chosen to enforce stricter standards than those of the EPA, but others allow higher levels of toxins in composts and a few have chosen not to regulate municipal solid waste composts at all. That leaves residents dependent on the integrity of the compost-processor, often a private contractor operating under severe budget constraints.

Another complication in assessing the dangers of compost contaminants is the mixed results that have emerged from various scientific studies (most of which were conducted in Europe, where composting has been an important element of the waste disposal system for half a century).

Although it is clear that heavy metals may accumulate in the soil as a result of mixed-waste compost application, in most cases they have not visibly impaired plant growth, nor have they typically accumulated in food crops to levels harmful to animals and man—although in two studies, calves that had composted MSW (with modest and legal levels of heavy metals contamination) included in their food showed significantly elevated lead levels in their livers, kidneys, and fat).[3] There are indications of more subtle damage: heavy metal accumulations that do not directly affect plants can sap their growth by poisoning the microscopic life of the soil. A Spanish study[4] found MSW composts unnaturally lacking in the bacteria that "fix"

---

[3]P. R. Utley, O. H. Jones, Jr., and W. C. McCormick, "Processed Municipal Solid Waste as a Roughage and Supplemental Protein Source in Beef Cattle Finishing Diets," *Journal of Animal Science*, 35, no. 1 (1972): 139–143; J. C. Johnson, Jr., P. R. Utley, R. L. Jones, and W. C. McCormick, "Aerobic Digested Municipal Garbage as a Feedstuff for Cattle," *Journal of Animal Science*, 41, no. 5 (1975): 1487–1495.

[4]M. Diaz-Ravina, M. J. Acea, and T. Carballas, "Microbiological Characterization of Four Composted Urban Refuses," *Biological Wastes*, 30 (1989): 89–100.

atmospheric nitrogen, making it available to plants. Several American researchers[5] have found an apparent decline of nitrogen fixation by various plants of the legume family — clovers and soybeans — when they were grown on soils treated with metals-contaminated composts.

Whether or not mixed-waste composts do pose a threat to the vigor and wholesomeness of food crops may be a moot question. In the Netherlands, farmers had been applying mixed waste compost to their fields for decades, but in the 1980s ceased to do so. At that time public concern about heavy metal contamination began affecting the value of the farmers' harvests, and when they as a group refused to buy compost, the municipalities were forced to switch to source separation.

This has proven very effective in controlling contaminants — it has reduced the lead content of the compost there by 80 percent (to 130 parts per million), for example, whereas the most elaborate mechanized separation systems for processing mixed wastes have only reduced the lead by 20 to 40 percent (leaving it as high as 680 ppm, more than twice the level the EPA deems

---

[5]S. P. McGrath, P. C. Brookes, and K. E. Giller, "Effects of Potentially Toxic Metals in Soil Derived from Past Applications of Sewage Sludge on Nitrogen Fixation by *Trifolium repens L.*," *Soil Biology and Biochemistry*, 20 (1988): 415–424; F. T. Bingham, A. L. Page, R. J. Mahler, and T. J. Ganje, "Yield and Cadmium Accumulation of Forage Species in Relation to Cadmium Content of Sludge Amended Soil," *Journal of Environmental Quality*, 5 (1976): 57–60; K. E. Giller, S. P. McGrath, and P. R. Hirsch, "Absence of Nitrogen Fixation in Clover Grown on Soil Subject to Long-term Contamination with Heavy Metals Is Due to Survival of Only Ineffective *Rhizobium*," *Soil Biology and Biochemistry*, 21 (1989): 841–848; J. A. Rother, J. W. Millbank, and I. Thornton, "Nitrogen Fixation by White Clover (*Trifolium repens*) in Grasslands on Soil Contaminated with Cadmium, Lead, and Zinc," *Journal of Soil Science*, 34 (1983): 127–136.

acceptable).[6] Currently, the Netherlands, Germany, Austria, and Switzerland have all embraced source-separated composting, and the European Economic Community has established a Composting Commission that promises to establish strict, membership-wide standards that will force other European composters to follow suit.

Commercial composters in the United States, those private companies who produce compost for profit, have already followed suit. They have found that while the EPA's system of NOAELs may protect the public, they have given mixed-waste compost a bad name. Potential customers—landscapers, for example, or nurserymen—have been reluctant to use any such product. Who wants to explain to customers that what you are spreading around their homes is "really quite an acceptable risk"?

That's why commercial composters have pursued a policy of *de facto* source separation. They take wastes mainly from industrial producers such as food processors and mix this with farm manures. The only municipal wastes they accept, generally, are yard trimmings. The businesspeople who run these plants understand that the customer's perception is as important as the actual quality of a product when you want to move it through the marketplace. ▪

---

[6]G. R. E. M. van Roosmalen, J. W. A. Lustenhouwer, J. Oosthoek, and M. M. G. Senden, "Heavy Metal Sources and Contamination Mechanisms in Compost Production," *Resources and Conservation*, 14 (1987): 321–334. An American study (L. de Gaere, "Successful Composting and Anaerobic Bioconversion of Biodegradable Plastics," *Proceedings of the 1990 National Conference on Standards for Compost Products*, Solid Waste Composting Conference, November 14–16, 1990, pp. 66–72) of four municipal composts in this country found the source-separated ones to average 88 percent less lead than the mixed-waste compost.

Austin — Flushed with Pride

Are there any municipal composters that are marketing their product successfully? Certainly — the Water and Wastewater Utility in Austin, Texas, has turned its "Dillo Dirt" into one of the region's real growth industries.

The utility had to do something with the black muck that settled out of waste-water in the course of treatment. Landfilling it is expensive (most cities in Texas pay $80–100 per dry ton in hauling and tipping fees) and the alternative — land spreading, which means applying the muck directly to the soil on farms — can be ticklish. Tell the neighbors that the smell drifting over the fence comes from "sewage sludge," and they won't be happy. Yes, it's been pasteurized and the pathogens are all dead — but that's not the point.

Anyway, what the treatment plants were collecting was too good to throw away. Because of Austin's aggressive campaigning with local industry to keep toxins out of the sewer system, the sludge is low in contaminants and, of course, rich in organics and nitrogen. This richness means any compost made with the sludge will reach a temperature fatal to germs, so they aren't a problem. In short, it's an ideal material.

Jim Doersam is the city engineer who has undertaken to do this, and in the process become "sludge reuse manager." Processing the sludge was easy. He mixed it with wood chips from tree trimming along the local power lines, then spread it in windrows that were turned and aerated periodically by machine — the process was developed by the EPA back in the early 1970s. But selling the results took imagination.

To allay public fears, Doersam decided to exceed federal safety regulations — though only required to test the compost for contaminants twice a year, he chose to test monthly and to make the results available to customers. The choice of names, too, was a good stroke, for "Dillo Dirt" sounds much more user friendly than "sludge," and it lends itself to a cute logo complete with overall-clad armadillo and wheelbarrow. Probably the crucial step that Doersam took, though, was that before ever trying to make a sale, he took care to create a market.

For two years, in 1987 and 1988, the utility donated its compost to various city projects: tree plantings along median strips, the renovation of soccer fields, an open-air concert site. These efforts won mentions in the local media, but the real publicity came with an incident that Doersam recalls as "sheer luck"—luck, that is, for the composters.

A city crew was renovating an area in a lakeside park when the wind changed. A pack of joggers were showered with the material spraying out of the city's manure spreader, and were furious when told that it was sewage sludge. They called the newspaper, the newspaper got in touch with Doersam (it must have been a slow day for news), and, seeing the humor in the situation perhaps, ran the story. Austin is a university town, and a community of great environmental conscience, so the public came down very much on the side of composters.

A demand for Dillo Dirt was growing—throughout 1988 the Wastewater Utility had been giving Dillo Dirt away to city employees and when their neighbors started lining up, to them as well. Yet Doersam still wasn't ready quite yet to set up his cash register. Instead, he held a meeting with local businesspeople who were already making and selling composts of various sorts. They threatened a smear campaign if the utility went into competition with them, either by selling directly to the public or by selling all its compost to a single distributor. But if the utility would wholesale its compost to all of them — or at least to anyone who chose to pay a modest registration fee — then that was . . . great.

Dillo Dirt fetches $7 per cubic yard for the utility now, and retails for $15–$25 delivered. It has become a mainstay of local gardeners, even Doersam, who told us he had just paid $110 for the 6 yards he needed to renovate his lawn. What had been a problem is a fast-growing (if modest) source of income. In 1989, the utility had sold just 2,074 cubic yards, realizing $12,136.68. In the first three months of 1993, it had already moved 4,848 yards, for a return of $36,319.34. "Business," the sludge reuse manager observed, "is great."

State of the Art

This is a period of tremendous, rapid changes in composting, and that scares investors. After all, no one wants to invest $13 million (the price of the average composting plant) into a clever-seeming concept that turns out a year or two later to be a technological dead end. It's a bit like buying a personal computer: you want to get the device of the future, but how can you tell?

We don't have any crystal ball, but we can read a form sheet and we are putting our money on the style of composting pioneered recently in Fairfield County, Connecticut.

This project was born of a disagreement between Jan Beyea, the chief scientist of the National Audubon Society, and representatives of Procter & Gamble, the Cincinnati-based corporate giant. They seemed to be on the same side: Audubon has been promoting community composting through public education and its local chapters, while Procter & Gamble has set aside $20 million to fund initiatives and research in this area. But Beyea believes firmly in source separation while P&G is just as definite in its support of mixed-waste recycling.

Their arguments, carried on in the forum of the National Recycling Coalition (NRC), threatened to block any progress toward advancing composting as a means of municipal waste disposal. So fellow NRC members made Beyea and P&G's Bruce Jones cochairs of the committee on composting and told them to resolve their differences.

Instead they agreed to disagree and then united in designing a pilot project that would satisfy them both.

What they settled on was neither source separated- or mixed-waste composting but a third method, the so-called wet-bag/dry-bag system of waste collection. In this, residents are encouraged to put recyclables and noncompostables into one container (the "dry" one), while food scraps, soiled paper, pet manures, and (yes!) disposable diapers are put into the "wet" one. Such a system involves fewer decisions for local residents and so is easier to implement. Although actually, since Beyea and Jones chose for their trials two communities with curbside recycling programs already in place, the two-bag collection system worked out more like a three- or four-bag system—glass and recyclable paper was already going into separate containers in Greenwich and Fairfield before the composters came to town.

The project planners chose these neighboring towns because of the strength of their existing recycling programs and their nearness to a sludge-and-yard-waste composting plant that could provide facilities. Another advantage was the presence in Greenwich of a strong Audubon chapter that could coordinate volunteers and provide onsite supervision. P&G supplied the funding: $250,000.

In February 1992, the project staff began contacting residents (via letter) asking for their voluntary participation, and by the beginning of March they had recruited about 400 households of participants, as well as three local McDonalds restaurants. Special bags for the disposal of wet garbage were distributed—made of brown paper lined with cellulose, these were water-proof yet readily biodegradable and had printed on their side instructions about what sorts of materials were to be included with the compostables. Animal-proof bins in which to store wet bags outdoors were also made available at no cost to participants, and an 800 number set up to handle questions.

Because the composting plant could not handle the extra wastes except temporarily, this project was de-signed as a demonstration only. On March 10, collec-tion of the compostables began, and on April 3 it ended. But during that 3½-week period, the composters achieved an unanticipated success.

Curbside recycling was already diverting 40 percent of the average household's trash — composting diverted an additional 30 percent (14 pounds per week), so that the total diversion from the incinerator or landfill was 70 percent. And this figure would have been higher had the experiment been conducted later in the year, during the growing season when many of the participating households would have been generating large quan-tities of compostable yard wastes. So the project spon-sors' claims of a 70-percent diversion were, in fact, conservative.

Collecting the organic wastes is all well and good, but what of their conversion into humus? After shred-ding, mixing with yard wastes (three parts trash to one part trimmings and leaves), and a thorough wetting (the moisture level was brought up to 50 percent), the compostables were loaded into enclosed, mechanically agitated and aerated bays for thirty days. Then the nearly mature compost was screened to remove any un-decomposed materials and piled outside in windrows for six weeks.

At the end came what is (for Tom at least) the proof of the pudding: half the finished compost (about 18.5 cubic yards) was taken to the Connecticut Agricultural Experiment Station for testing. It assayed well below the permissible levels for heavy metals—the lead content, for instance, was less than 92 parts per million, less than a third of the EPA's NOAEL, while mercury tested at less than one-eighth of the NOAEL, and cadmium less than one-thirtieth. Most important, it grew beautiful tomatoes. When spread over fields at a rate of 50 tons per acre, it incrased the harvest by 38 percent. Each plant produced an average of 25 percent more fruit, and each tomato weighed on average 11 percent more.

No one has to explain the importance of that to a gardener— or to a hungry neighbor, either. Anyone can understand the importance of healthy, fertile soil and of renewing our abused farmlands, yards, and parks. But it may take some re-education to arrive at those goals. For all of us. We were priding ourselves on our compost consciousness not long ago when we called Richard Kashmanian at the EPA's Office of Policy, Planning and Evaluation. We were asking him about composting as a means of solid waste disposal when he interrupted and courteously but firmly bawled us out.

"Can I suggest that in your writing you should not say that composting is a way to dispose of wastes? That sends the wrong message. Not only are leaves and grass [or chicken bones either, for that matter] not wastes, but composting is a way to *manage* them, not dispose of them. Disposal is what goes on in the landfill."

So if we are planning for renewal, we better start looking at our resources in a new and positive way. We promise not to call the materials of rebirth "waste" and "trash" in the future. You must do the same.

A Bumper Crop

It's been fifty years at least since America wrote off the family farm—"too small, too labor intensive, can't compete in the international marketplace." Those small acreages that do persist in nearly every region of the country are testaments mainly to the brutal hard work, personal sacrifice, and pigheaded stubbornness of the proprietors. Now, though, those holdouts may be about to reap their reward. America's towns are discovering that if they want to compost their organic wastes, they may need the farmers' help.

Typically, town planners have viewed farms mainly as raw material, empty space over which suburbs can sprawl. For their part, farmers view suburbanization with considerable apprehension. It may increase the dollar value of their land, but that benefits them only when they sell out, and in the meantime taxes increase and the new residents continually complain about the noise of farm machinery, the dust, and, above all, the smell of the manure. Sure, cows and pigs and chickens and horses are cute, but they aren't sanitary.

However, livestock is what makes farm and suburb such a neat fit from the composter's point of view. Animal waste is nitrogenous, whereas the suburb's bulkiest organic wastes—leaves and tree trimmings—are carbonaceous. The two go together like cookies and milk.

There's more to the fit than just that. Municipal governments are equipped for waste collection and delivery. They have the necessary trucks and personnel, and budgets to pay by the ton for waste disposal. Farmers, in contrast, have the space to compost and most of the equipment necessary for building and managing industrial-sized heaps. They even have a use for the product—it can replace fertilizer in their fields—and the machinery to spread it. Besides, farmers have been composting to a greater or lesser extent ever since we cut the trees and busted the sod. Composting is something farmers of small acreages know and understand.

Over the last few years, there have been many instances of farmers moving into this new kind of waste disposal. We had been reading accounts of Maine farmers who were taking a couple of tons of old directories from the telephone company every week, shredding them for use as bedding in their dairy barns, and then composting them once they were soiled. There was the dairy farmer in a New York suburb who was accepting old newspapers from a nearby town for the same purpose. There was another dairyman who was taking corrugated cardboard from a shoe factory.

Initially, the benefit to the farmers was that the new source of bedding freed them from the need either to buy or grow straw. That can be a considerable savings, too, since one cow will soil 1,332 pounds of straw in a single year. But through decades of hard times American farmers have developed a well-honed instinct for sources of extra income and it didn't take them long to see the possibilities of this situation.

The farmer in Maine was soon taking food waste from a local supermarket to add to his soiled cardboard, and he was selling the extra compost this generated to landscapers. Another fellow near the coast began taking mussel shells from a shellfish packager and charging $35 per ton for the privilege. It's the man down the road from Tom, though, the fellow who let the City of Middletown dump 1,200 loads of leaves under his cows, who represents the real future of this new kind of agriculture.

That's what the Rodale Institute believes, at any rate. This research organization grew out of a 68-acre farm that J. I. Rodale bought in 1941 to ensure his family's food supply through the shortages of World War II.

Composting was a key to Rodale's restoration of his wornout fields, and it remains a central part of the institute's efforts to develop farming and gardening systems that regenerate (rather than deplete) natural resources.

In recent years, the institute has worked with the USDA to promote on-farm composting, focusing specifically on developing methods for cocomposting rural and urban wastes. Politics can make strange bedfellows, and this association between government specialists and the antichemical advocate (J. I. Rodale was also the founder of *Organic Gardening* magazine and America's greatest apostle of the organic movement) may seem unlikely. But if the USDA was to put into practice its new Low-Input Sustainable Agriculture program (LISA—a part of the 1990 farm bill), it needed access to a new constituency, and it needed a partner that could speak the language.

With its experience in working with operators of small farms, the institute knew that developing composting recipes wasn't enough. The composters would need an agent to help them reach clients and organize an industry. So the institute extended its original brief and in the fall of 1991 through the winter of 1992 conducted a study of opportunities of cocomposting in the four counties around its Kutztown, Pennsylvania, base.

Surveying sixty municipalities in Berks, Lancaster, Lehigh, and Northampton counties—a place where suburbs are infiltrating what has traditionally been rich farmlands—institute personnel interviewed town and city officials to identify their composting needs. Then it assembled focus groups of administrators, politicians, and farmers to identify obstacles.

What the focus groups revealed was that the farmers shrank from any activity that involved dealing with more government regulation, and they knew that composting on a commercial scale would bring all the various agencies that deal with waste management down on their heads. The institute is easing that situation by bringing representatives of all the agencies together to formulate a single, nonconflicting set of composting regulations, and by donating its services in writing regulations that will be intelligible to farmers. It is also pushing to have the regulations administered through the state Department of Agriculture, one agency that farmers know and trust.

Meanwhile, the focus groups also revealed that municipalities typically lacked any means of contacting potential cocomposters. In response to this, the institute has been developing two computer data bases. One lists municipalities that are working with or are interested in working with composters, so that the institute can refer farmers to customers. The other data base is a statewide index of farm composters, with information about what they are currently composting, the volume of materials they handle, what price they charge for finished compost (if they sell it), and whether they test the results. This the institute is publishing in book form as a guide that will circulate via county Cooperative Extension agents.

When we spoke to Cary Oshins, the institute's technical manager and the supervisor of the cocomposting projects, he took care not to claim too much credit. Still, he noted that since the institute undertook this work, three farmers in Berks County and several more in Northampton have started taking in municipal wastes, while Lancaster County has chosen this as its principal means of yard waste disposal and is actively promoting this type of town–farm partnership through the county Solid Waste Authority.

The institute calculates that cocomposting is profitable for the farmers at tipping fees of as little as $1 to

$5 per cubic yard. That price will cover the expense of handling, and the profits will come from reduced bills for fertilizer or from sales of finished compost. Currently Cary Oshins is developing a detailed profile of startup costs to help sell cocomposting to farmers.

This process is not right for every town, Oshins freely admits, but could save money for many. Yet he has met with one worry that has nothing to do (at least directly) with dollars and cents. In a report he quoted the city recycling coordinator who feared that cocomposting "creates a dependence on farmers, leaving the municipality vulnerable if the farm should stop accepting leaves or be sold to developers." Which may be the point.

Compost This Book

IT'S A BEAUTIFUL fall day. The temperature is in the sixties. There's a nice cool breeze blowing from the northwest. You're feeling pretty good because you just had a fabulous lunch of asparagus with cheese, cucumber salad, and the last of those great tomatoes with some olive oil and a little basil.

All the crops were great this year because in the spring you were smart enough to buy a little book that told you everything you needed to know about the secrets of composting. You're feeling pretty rich too. Maybe not rich enough to buy that new Lexus, but at least a couple of hundred dollars further in the black from all the unnecessary fertilizer and lawn food that you DIDN'T buy.

The leaves have just started to fall and you've been dutifully gathering them up, mixing them with grass

226

clippings and stuff from the kitchen—you can hardly wait for the cycle to begin again. You stroll off to the living room and browse through the book again to see if there's anything you've forgotten from last season. Lo and behold, you know it ALL. You know the right proportions of everything to use. You know how much wet, how much dry, how to check the temperature, which bin works best, and just about everything else. You also know that if you say one more word about composting to your friends, you will never be invited to a party again.

So what to do with your trusty old book. You could, of course, keep it for reference or pass it on to a friend. But then you remember something from the very beginning of the book—that little line about the book being printed on recycled paper with soy-based ink. Could you? Would you? Isn't there something sacrilegious about destroying a book?

Naaahhh. . . . Go ahead. First pull off the cover and throw that away (we *told* you that glossy paper wasn't good for the heap). Rip out the pages and discard the binding (we couldn't find a wholesome organic glue for that—it's up to you to create a market by promising to buy and compost *lots* more copies). Then comes the fun.

Tear the loose pages into lots of nice little pieces. Mix them in with the coffee grounds and the leaves and the grass clippings. You're an expert now, so you no longer need the instruction book. And nothing would make the authors happier than to know that they've not only taught you how to have a better garden, but now they're actually a part of that garden.

It's been great fun sharing the secrets of composting with our friends. And now we are about to become part of the process itself.

The cycle of life goes on. And on. And on.

Composting Bins, Tools, and Supplies

We strongly recommend that before buying any compost equipment you visit the National Home Composting Park at the American Horticultural Society headquarters, River Farm, 7931 East Boulevard Drive, Alexandria, VA 22308. There you'll see any bin you can imagine (and some you couldn't) actually in operation. If you can't visit, write for the free fact sheet about models and suppliers, and be sure to enclose a legal size, stamped, and self-addressed envelope.

A. M. Leonard, Inc.

P.O. Box 816
Piqua, OH 45356
Supplier of tools to the horticultural industry; Tom wouldn't buy a manure fork (or any other gardening tool) from anyone else. Free catalogue.

Bricker's Organic Farm, Inc.

824-K Sandbar Ferry Road
Augusta, GA 30901
Source of Kricket Krap and decomposition-enhancing yucca soap, the "Quick Composter," and an extensive list of handbooks on various aspects of composting. The T-shirts are sure to inspire double-takes.

CanDo Composter

5990 Old Stilesboro Road
Acworth, GA 30101
Manufacturer of Marty's favorite rotating drum composter— that recycled barrel does the job, and it costs maybe a third of the glitzier competitors. Good value. Free brochure.

Environmental Applied Products

2029 North 23rd Street
Boise, ID 83702
Manufacturer of the Tumble Bug, a giant, free-standing plastic icosahedral (20-sided) bin. Roll the thing around the yard, and it tosses and aerates the compostables inside — Joe Keyser at the National Home Composting Park assured us it works, and the inventor later explained why it's a good buy. According to him, its large capacity (20 cubic feet) means that the per unit compost cost is much lower than that of any barrel-type compost tumblers. That's great, but we must admit that for us the main attraction is that the Tumble Bug is so much fun. Could double as outdoor sculpture.

Garden Way Manufacturing Company, Inc.

102nd Street & 9th Avenue
Troy, NY 12180
Manufacturer of the E-Z Spin Tumbler as well as top-of-the-line chipper-shredders. If you are going to invest in one of those high-priced beasts, you might as well get the best.

Gardener's Eden

P.O. Box 7307
San Francisco, CA 94120
Check out the Solar Composter; and the sensibly priced but oh-so-chic French Garden Gloves should be a lifesaver for the composter with soft hands.

Gardener's Supply

128 Intervale Road
Burlington, VT 05401
Manufacturer of an inexpensive wire compost bin, as well as the pricier Green Magic Tumbler and (for those with a yearning for invertebrate pets) an indoor worm compost bin. Also sells compost thermometers and aerator tools. Free catalogue.

Gardens Alive!

5100 Schenley Place
Lawrenceburg, IN 47025
No-nonsense catalogue of supplies for organic gardeners — includes the Compost Digester bin (what they call "the Cad-

illac of compost bins," but then they've never seen Tom's homemade one) and red worms.

Kemp Co.

160 Koser Road
Lititz, PA 17543
Manufacturer of Kemp Compost Tumbler and Kemp Shredder/Chippers—all made in the United States, sold direct by mail order. Will let you test their bin for two free batches; not bad. Write, or call 800-441-5367 for free catalogue.

Lescha North America

P.O. Box 266
Bolton, Ontario, Canada L0P 1A0
North American manufacturer of the Ro-Si "state-of-the-art compost tumbler"—a European import, the SAAB Turbo of bins.

Ringer Research

9959 Valley View Road
Eden Prairie, MN 55344
All sorts of composting and organic gardening products—distributed through local retail outlets. For a complete list of products, write for brochure.

Rubbermaid

Manufacturer of the Double-Wall Composter, insulated bin for through-the-winter composting. Order through local garden center or hardware store.

Smith & Hawken

25 Corte Madera
Mill Valley, CA 94941
Don't be fooled by the upscale catalogue; this is a good source of well-made tools and equipment, all reasonably priced (considering the quality of the product). Source of Biostack Composter and compost-aerating tool, as well as lots of fashionable (and yes, well-made) compost-wear (Tom wouldn't compost without his Panama hat, Marty swears by his clogs). Free catalogue.

SolarCone, Inc.
P.O. Box 67
Seward, IL 61077
U.S. distributor of the Green Cone, our favorite off-the-rack bin and the only one we recommend for composting meat scraps. Write for brochure, or call 800-80-Solar.

Swisher Mower & Machine Co, Inc.
333 E. Gay Street
P.O. Box 67
Warrensburg, MO 64093
Swisher's solar-powered compost tumblers can process up to 23 bushels of compostables at once (smallest model has 12-bushel capacity)—comes complete with solar panels to power the automated tumbling system. Write for brochure.

Further Reading on Composting Issues and Techniques*

The Complete Book of Composting. Emmaus, PA: Rodale Books, 1974. Interesting material on the history of composting, almost 1,000 pages of information about carbon–nitrogen ratios, and so on. We prefer this classic edition to subsequent ones.

Composting to Reduce the Waste Stream. Ithaca, NY: Northeast Regional Agricultural Engineering Service, 1991.

Disposal of Household Hazardous Waste. Ithaca, NY: Cornell University Resource Center. Keeping hazardous waste out of your garbage (or at least out of the organic portion of it) is crucial to the quality of any municipal compost your community might make. For a complete listing of domestic hazardous wastes and suggestions about appropriate methods of

---

*Many of the books in this and the following list are currently out of print. They are available through interlibrary loan, however, and are in many respects more informative than anything you'll find in the bookstore today (with the exception of our book, of course).

disposal, send $1.00 to Cornell University Resource Center, 7-8 BTP, Ithaca, NY 14850 and ask for the pamphlet cited above.

On-Farm Composting Handbook. Ithaca, NY: Northeast Regional Agricultural Engineering Service, 1992.

Gershuny, Grace, and Joseph Smillie. *The Soul of the Soil: A Guide to Ecological Soil Management.* 2nd ed. St. Johnsbury, VT: Gaia Services, 1986. A wonderful title and a most practical book. Aimed at farmers but useful for backyard growers, too.

Golueke, Dr. Clarence G. *Composting: A Study of the Process and Its Principles.* Emmaus, PA: Rodale Press, 1972. Still the clearest and most concise scientific treatment of composting. Makes the natural processes intelligible to the lay reader.

Schatz, Albert, and Vivian Schatz. *Teaching Science with Garbage.* Emmaus, PA: Rodale Press, 1971. Lends a special relevance to schoolroom lessons in science, mathematics, and social studies.

Stephenson, W. A. *Seaweed in Agriculture and Horticulture.* London: Faber & Faber, Ltd., 1968. If you live near a coast and aren't composting seaweed, you are cheating your garden. Check this book out and see what Marty is missing.

Magazines for the Modern Composter

Biocycle, J. G. Press, Inc., 419 State Avenue, Emmaus, PA 18049; a monthly magazine that offers a professional perspective on solid waste management in lay language.

Garbage, 2 Main Street, Gloucester, MA 01930; billing itself as "the practical journal for the environment," this magazine takes a lively and informed look at issues surrounding waste reduction, recycling, and disposal—"muckraking" is a particularly appropriate description in this case. Published six times a year.

Further Reading on Our Composting Heritage

Bagley, William Chandler. *Soil Erosion and the Civil War.* Washington, DC: American Council on Public Affairs, 1942. Could

America's most terrible conflict have been averted by composting? Probably not, but this book (originally written as a doctoral thesis) makes very clear the cost of mistreating the soil.

Browne, D. J. *The Field Book of Manures; or, The American Muck Book.* New York: C. M. Saxton, 1854. Directions for composting everything from blubber to tree bark.

Fessenden, Thomas G. *The Husbandman and Housewife.* Bellows Falls, VT: Bill Blake & Co., 1820. Recipes for Yankee composting.

Howard, Albert. *An Agricultural Testament.* London: Oxford University Press, 1940. The scripture for the organic gardening movement. Later composters have improved on some of Howard's methods, but his indictment of modern agriculture rings truer than ever: "Mother earth deprived of her manurial rights is in revolt; the land is going on strike."

King, F. H. *Farmers of Forty Centuries.* Emmaus, PA. Organic Gardening Press, 1948. A fascinating survey of composting's role in traditional East Asian agriculture.

Johnson, Samuel W. *Essays on Peat, Muck and Commercial Manures.* Hartford, CT: Brown & Gross, 1859. Johnson was the father of scientific agriculture in the United States and the first to put composting on a scientific basis. This book still makes interesting reading.

Storl, Wolf D. *Culture and Horticulture.* Wyoming, RI: Bio-Dynamic Literature, 1979. A guide to anthroposophical composting, with chapter titles such as "Magical Weather Control" and "Transmutation, Destruction and Creation of Matter"— a radically different insight.

Washington, Jefferson, Lincoln and Agriculture. Washington, DC: Bureau of Agricultural Economics, U.S. Department of Agriculture, 1937. Writings on composting, from the Founding Fathers.

Further Reading on Community Composting

The Biocycle Guide to Yard Waste Composting. Emmaus, PA: J. G. Press, 1989. Essential reading for anyone who wants to start a municipal yard waste composting program.

Municipal Solid Waste Composting: A Viable Disposal Option for Connecticut? Cornwall Bridge, CT: Housatonic Valley Association, 1991. A concise but detailed consideration of the issues, of relevance to any community investigating this option. Obtainable by writing to the Housatonic Valley Association, P.O. Box 28, Cornwall Bridge, CT 06754.

Organizations Offering Advice and Help to Community Composters

Composting Council
114 South Pitt Street
Alexandria, VA 22314
703-739-2401
An industrial organization formed to promote composting as a means of solid waste reduction; membership includes large corporations such as Procter & Gamble, commercial composters, academics, and public officials. Besides serving as a clearinghouse for information from all sources, the council is pursuing its own research in areas such as potential markets for compost and standards for composts.

Environmental Defense Fund
1875 Connecticut Avenue, N.W.
Washington, DC 20009
A watchdog group with reservations about the benefits and safety of community composting; its position papers offer a useful counterbalance to the optimistic claims of commercial composting firms.

Master Composter Program
c/o Seattle Tilth Association
4649 Sunnyside Avenue North
Seattle, WA 98103
Can help community groups form local chapters of this very effective educational program. Write for information, and enclose $2 and a legal size, self-addressed, stamped envelope.

National Audubon Society
700 Broadway
New York, NY 10003
Can provide information about the very successful wet-bag/dry-bag composting demonstration project conducted in Greenwich and Fairfield, Connecticut, in the spring of 1992.

Rodale Institute
611 Siegfriedale Road
Kutztown, PA 19530
The research organization with the most experience in all aspects of composting; a leader in promoting on-farm composting as a means of municipal waste disposal.

Worms (if you must)

Appelhof, Mary. *Worms Eat My Garbage.* Kalamazoo, MI: Flower Press, 1982. A practical guide to vermi-composting.

Darwin, Charles R. *The Formation of Vegetable Mould Through the Action of Worms, with Observations on Their Habits.* University of Chicago Press (Chicago, 1985). The great man kept worms in his study to study their response to everything from lights of varying intensities, to his piano playing. Then he wrote this, the classic study on earthworms' role in decomposition and the renewal of the soil. Worthwhile reading even for vermiphobes such as Tom and Marty.

Carter Worm Farm
Plains, GA 31780
A good source for "Pure Bred Hybrid Red Wigglers" (in lots of up to 100,000 worms) and "Fishbait Literature," too. Free catalogue.

INDEX

236